Living Lulav

MOSAICA PRESS

Living Lulav

DISCOVERING OURSELVES
THROUGH THE MITZVAH OF
THE FOUR SPECIES

—

BINYAMIN FELDMAN

לזכר נשמות

In memory of

הרב יוסף בן הרב מנחם ושפרה
ורעיתו שיינא גאלדא בת הרב חיים יואל ושרה רבקה

Rabbi and Mrs. Joseph H. Feldman

———

דוד בן משה וחנה ביילה
ורעיתו פייגא שבע בת ישראל דוד וגאלדא בלומא

Mr. and Mrs. David Samber

———

עמרם הלל בן מנחם ואסתר

Amram Hillel Feldman

In memory of our beloved parents

חיים דוב בן יצחק אייזק ז״ל

מלכה בת שמואל זאב ז״ל

יחיאל בן הרב יוסף יהודה הלוי ז״ל

שיינדל בת ישראל יואל ז״ל

SANDY AND LILLIAN SHAPIRO

TEL. (718) 520-0115
FAX (718) 268-0186

קהל נחלת יצחק ד'הומנא
CONGREGATION NACHLAS YITZCHOK
141-43 73RD AVENUE
KEW GARDENS, HILLS, N. Y. 11367

NOACH ISAAC OELBAUM
RABBI
AUTHOR OF SEFORIM
MINCHAS CHEN

נח אייזיק אהעלבוים
בעהמח"ס מנחת חן
רב ואב"ד דק"ק נחלת יצחק
בקיו גארדענס הילס, נ. י.

בס"ד

[handwritten Hebrew text]

Rabbi Zev Leff

Rabbi of Moshav Matityahu
Rosh HaYeshiva—Yeshiva Gedola Matityahu

הרב זאב לף

מרא דאתרא מושב מתתיהו
ראש הישיבה—ישיבה גדולה מתתיהו

D.N. Modiin 71917   **Tel: 08-976-1138** טל'   **Fax: 08-976-5326** פקס'   ד.נ. מודיעין 71917

Dear Friends,

I have read the manuscript "Living Lulav - Discovering Ourselves Through the Mitzvah of the Four Species" by Rabbi Binyamin Feldman.

The author presents a truly fascinating and comprehensive understanding of ideas inherent in the mitzvah of the four species. Although the basic reason we fulfill mitzvos is to fulfill G-d's will which is beyond our comprehension, just as the reason we eat various foods that are nutritous is because that is how G-d created us and the world. Athough we can discuss the what and how concerning nutrition, the why remains in the mystery of G-d's will. However, G-d endowed food with color, taste and aroma to enhance our eating experience. So too, mitzvos have tastes, aromas and colors that we can sense on many levels both intellectually, emotionally and spiritually, that make the mitzvah edyfying and impact not only on our essence but on our conscience, behavior, and experience.

The author weaves a truly magnificent explanation of the three aspects of this mitzvah, joy, beauty, and life, into a beautiful tapestry that makes the mitzvah truly meaningful and inspiring.

Aside from the main purpose of the book to present a deeper perspective in this specific mitzvah, it also serves to make one aware of the vast and deep meaning in all mitzvos and gives one a desire to plumb the depths of Torah knowledge to discover these treasures.

I found the work lucid, easily understood even to one not well versed in Torah. The complex ideas are developed in a very logical progression and presented in an interesting and inspiring manner, and based on solid and authentic Torah sources.

I recommend this work as a valuable tool and aid in performing the mitzvah of the four species and familarizing one with the depths of Torah thought.

I commend Rabbi Feldman for a truly quality presentation. I pray that Hashem Yisborach bless him and his family with life, health, and the wherewithal to continue to merit the community.

Sincerely,
With Torah blessings

Rabbi Zev Leff

Rabbi Yitzchak Berkovits
Sanhedria HaMurchevet 113/27
Jerusalem, Israel 97707
02-5813847

יצחק שמואל הלוי ברקוביץ
ראש רשת הכוללים לינת הצדק
סנהדרי״ה המורחבת 113/27
ירושלם ת״ו

בס״ד ירושלם ת״ו כ׳ סיון תשע״א

Living Lulav is not a collection of fluffy sermons aimed at giving the reader positive feelings towards a mitzva little understood.

This sefer is the work of Hagaon Rav Binyamin Yair Feldman whose intellectual honesty has little tolerance for anything lacking authenticity. Every idea presented is carefully sourced and expressed true to the original.

Yes, the reader will learn to understand what he is doing in waving the four species and will be given the opportunity to "live" the mitzva as intended.

May this be the first of many such works of the author, and may he enlighten Torah to the masses with his brilliance and authenticity.

ברכה,

יצחק ברקוביץ

מוסדות אור שמח מרכז טננבאום ע.ר. 00-21343-00-58
רח' שמעון הצדיק 22-28 ירושלים ת.ד. 18103
טל: 02-581-0315

Michtav Bracha

Shvat 5781

Every Orthodox Jew, and quite a few non-Orthodox Jews, are familiar with the mitzva of taking the Four Species on Sukkos. Many are even familiar with the beloved Midrashim correlating the species to different parts of the human body or different types of Jews. But at the end of the day, the simple, basic meaning of what we are doing remains elusive; what are we trying to accomplish when we shake various plants and a citrus fruit in various directions? What does Hashem want us to accomplish?

Rabbi Binyamin Feldman has written a truly fascinating book exploring these questions, basic questions that we often fail to even think about. He proposes an intriguing thesis that each species is intended to elicit a certain emotion of aesthetic joy which corresponds to a parallel spiritual dimension. The combination of these joys, like a well-arranged bouquet of flowers (a well-placed metaphor of the author), produces a cumulative effect that is greater and deeper than the sum of its individual parts.

The sefer is well written and lucidly organized. Solidly rooted in authentic Torah sources, it is at the same time a creative and innovative work. Most importantly, it will enable the reader to perform a vital, precious, beautiful mitzva with greater awareness and transformative effect and will give him/her a glimpse into the infinite depth of Hashem's Torah.

May Rabbi Feldman have much hatzlacha in the dissemination of this work and in all his avodas hakodesh.

B'virkas HaTorah,
**Yitzchak A. Breitowitz
Rav, Kehillas Ohr Somayach
Yerushalayim**

קהילה קדושה רמת אשכול
רח' פאראן, ירושלים

הרב שמואל יצחק צוקער
מרא דאתרא

בס"ד

עש"ק פ' שלח תשפ"א

הנני בזה בשבחה המגיע לכתבים של ידיד נפשי היקר, חריף ובקי טובא, מלא וגדוש על כל גדותיו בתורה
וביר"ש, הרה"ג ר' בנימין יאיר פלדמן שליט"א, המפאר את בית מדרשינו פעיה"ק באצילות,
בעדינות נפשו עם הארת פנים לכל אחד ואחד להשיב מענה לשואליו בדברי תורה והלכה מתוך נעימות
ועמות חן, ומקדיש שם שטים בהליכותיו בהצנע לכת, וכעת בעניוותנותו כי רבה, הגיש לפני את חיבורו פרי
עמלו על עניני ד' טינים, עם בקשתו שאצרף לזה הסכמתי הדלה.

מתוך עיון בדבריו ניכרת ההשקעה העצומה בהכנת החיבור, לבאר היסודות הפנימיים של קיום מצות ד'
טינים, בחדקק עצמו, בליבון כל פרט מפרטי המצוה בהרחבה ובטוב טעם ודעת, ובמשנתו רב עלה בידו
להפשיט יסודות עמוקים ונסתרים וללבנם באופן שיהיו ערבים על לבו של הלומד, גם למי שטים טעם
טעמה של פנימיות התורה, להחדיר השמחה והחיות בקיום העבודה.

ללא ספק יביא חיבורו הנפלא תועלת רב לדורשי ה' מבקשי תורה ודעת למצוא מענה ומהרחות בדורנו
דור עני, לקבל חיות ושמחה בכלל עבודת השי"ת, ולהלהיב את הלב מעצם הידיעה על היות נשמה בקרב
עם הנבחר, כמבואר היטב בחיבורו את הליימוד מהערבה להיות האדם שמח בחלקו גם כשמרגיש חסרון
ההשגה במדרגות ובמעלות העבודה.

ואצרף ברכתי מכל הלב, מתוך ידידות והערצה עמוקה, שיזכה להמשיך בדרכי הנעלים, להגות בתורה
הקדושה מתוך הרחבה ויישוב הדעת, להשפיע ממעייניו הברוכים להרוות צמאי עם בני ישראל, לזכות
את הרבים בכתביו ובחיבוריו מתוך נחת וכל טוב.

ידידך הדוש"ט בלו"נ

שמואל יצחק צוקער

שמואל ר' יצחק צוקער

CT. 191 Buitenkant Street, Vredehoek
JHB. 58 Oaklands Road, Orchards
P. Box 46559, Orange Grove, 2119

**OFFICE OF
THE CHIEF RABBI
OF SOUTH AFRICA**

CT. + 27 (0)21 461 6310 JHB. + 27 (0)10 214 2603
E. office@thechiefrabbi.co.za
W. chiefrabbi.co.za

Date 09/06/2021

In authoring *Living Lulav*, Rabbi Binyamin Feldman has performed a great service for *klal Yisroel* in drawing out the deeper meaning of this mitzvah.

Ultimately, we do the mitzvos because we are instructed to by Hashem, but at the same time He wants us to fully engage with the mitzvah so that we can become inspired, educated, uplifted and illuminated through the experience.

The Ramban in his commentary on the Chumash (Devarim 22:6) guides us on this path of approaching mitzvos. He explains that although it is beyond our grasp to plumb the depths of the Divine motivation behind any mitzvah, we are called on to discover the ways that Hashem gave for the mitzvah to purify, refine, elevate and transform us. This is what Rabbi Feldman has done so well with the mitzvah of *lulav* in this book – he has uncovered the wisdom of generations of great Torah scholars who help us to reveal glimpses of the Divine light that shines through the mitzvah. He structures their ideas beautifully into themes and demonstrates how these themes are immediately relevant to us in our journey of elevating ourselves.

May Hashem bless Rabbi Feldman with much success in his book. May it touch the hearts and minds of Jews all over the world and re-inspire us with this great mitzvah from Hashem.

With blessings,

Chief Rabbi Warren Goldstein

Table of Contents

SECTION III

Vivacity Reclaimed

Acknowledgments

Thanking the Creator for His kindnesses is no small matter, and I hope and pray to be worthy of expressing true gratitude for the myriad and unfathomable kindness that I have been blessed with, including the opportunity to hopefully stimulate deeper thought into the mitzvah of the Four Species and concepts derived from it.

The path to authentic gratitude to Hakadosh Baruch Hu begins with *hakaras hatov* to other human beings. It is my pleasure to thank the following individuals who had a part, directly or indirectly, in this book:

My parents, Rabbi Ilan and Rebbetzin Miriam Feldman, for their superhuman efforts, patience, and wisdom in raising me, and for their dedication to and belief in me; for their review of a very early draft of this work, and their invaluable comments, input, and ongoing encouragement of this project; and for their generous assistance in the publication of this book.

My in-laws, Rabbi Binyamin and Mrs. Tova Spiro, for serving as role models for us in their unwavering commitment to Torah and *chessed*; for their incredible dedication, support, and generosity to us as a family, and involvement with each of our children individually; and for the many important lessons and values that we have absorbed from them.

My grandparents, Rabbi Emanuel and Rebbetzin Estelle Feldman, for their care, generosity, example, and presence in our lives; and for their generous sponsorship of a very significant portion of this book to honor the memory of their parents (my great-grandparents, Rabbi and

Mrs. Joseph Feldman, *z"l*, and Mr. and Mrs. Dovid Samber, *z"l*); and their unforgettable son (my uncle), Amram Hillel Feldman, *z"l*.

Our Uncle Sandy and Aunt Lillian Shapiro, whose lives of *chessed* and dedication serve as examples for us and the entire extended family, for their generous sponsorship of a very significant portion of this book to honor the memory of their parents, *z"l*; for conveying to us the legacy of our Zaidy and Bubby Spiro, *z"l*; as well as for taking a personal interest in the development and well-being of our family.

My wife, Ruchama, for everything, and for her moral support at critical junctures during this project; our children, Shaindy, Shmuel Yaakov, Avraham, Refael Yehudah, Sarah'le, and Cheli, for the privilege of parenthood and so much else.

All of our siblings and their families, for making us proud and for being a part of our lives; my brother, Dr. Aharon Matis Feldman and his family, for their assistance in putting out this book.

The late Rabbi Leib Mintzberg for his classic work *Ben Melech*, which forms the foundation upon which the first section of this book is built, and which served as the catalyst for the writing of this entire work.

Rabbi Yechiel Schustal, in conversation with whom many of the ideas in this book were first conceived, for his insights, encouragement, general friendship, and advice on this book and everything else.

Members of Rabbi Schustal's Kollel Simchas Eliyahu, for sitting through a five-month series on the Arba Minim and for their input into clarifying the ideas; Rabbi Yechiel Greenblatt, then *meishiv* and *menahel* of the Kollel, for his enthusiasm and encouragement; R' Eli Tendler, a sterling member of the Kollel, for his ongoing interest.

Various groups at the Jerusalem Kollel, with which I am fortunate to be affiliated, for their input into clarifying these ideas; the entire staff and student body for their friendship and inspiration; Rabbi Yaakov Blackman, executive director of the Kollel, for his care and concern; Rabbi Josh Boretsky, for his intensive and ongoing efforts in keeping the Kollel going.

Mv"r, Rabbi Yitzchak Berkovits, for over twenty years of Torah, wisdom, and direction, and numerous other kindnesses to me, and for reviewing and writing a *haskamah* for this work; Rebbetzin Berkovits and their family, for their full partnership with Rabbi Berkovits in dedication to the *klal*.

Rabbi Yossi Stilerman, for his interest and appreciation of this project almost since its inception, and for everything I have learned from him; R' Yehoshua Lewin, for his ongoing encouragement and for modeling the excitement and joy of discovery.

Rabbi Noach Isaac Oelbaum, Rabbi Zev Leff, Rabbi Yitzchak Breitowitz, and South Africa Chief Rabbi Warren Goldstein, each of whom took time from their busy schedules to review the manuscript of this book, give feedback and *chizuk*, and write letters of *haskamah*.

Rabbi Shmuel Zucker, Rav of Kehillah Kedoshah of Ramat Eshkol (founded and ably directed by R' Daniel Green), for his appreciation and encouragement of this work; for taking the time to review this work and to write a letter of *haskamah*; and for serving as a beacon of light of the inner dimensions of Torah, true *avodah*, and fiery love for Hashem, Torah, and Klal Yisrael.

The publishers of Mosaica Press, Rabbi Yaacov Haber and Rabbi Doron Kornbluth, both of whom I have long admired for their inspiring roles in *harbatzas Torah* and Jewish education, for seeing the potential of this work; Rabbi Kornbluth, with whom I was in direct contact, for his enthusiasm, advice, and guidance.

All of the fantastic staff at Mosaica Press, whose meticulous and thoughtful editing, copyediting, proofreading, and designing immeasurably enhanced and transformed this volume.

Introduction

This book is about so much more than the Arba Minim.[1] True, our starting point is the mitzvah of the Four Species, which is practically relevant for only one week out of the year. But the discoveries to be made in the nooks and crannies of that mitzvah can meaningfully impact our approach to Torah and mitzvos throughout the year.

Inasmuch as our journey begins by analyzing the meaning of a particular mitzvah, it would seem we are foraying into the field of *taamei ha'mitzvos*, the "reasons" for the mitzvos. This field has long been fraught with tension. Proponents of its study point to the heightened sense of connection with, and passion for, mitzvos that it can foster. Detractors object on the grounds that it may create the impression that our fealty to Hashem's commandments is contingent upon our understanding and appreciating them, which is, of course, patently false.

There are, of course, ample precedents among the Rishonim for in-depth investigation of the rationales behind the mitzvos. Moreover, anecdotal evidence suggests that in today's world, the need for such study is simply undeniable. Nevertheless, as we hope to demonstrate, the course of study we take in this book is best described not as a quest for the rationale behind the mitzvah of the Arba Minim, but an

---

1   Throughout this work we have used the term "Arba Minim," which is simpler and more widely accepted than the more accurate "Arba'ah Minim."

1

investigation of its very nature and essence. Rather than demanding an explanation for why we should fulfill this mitzvah—the correct explanation being, of course, that God has so commanded us—we attempt to respond to the Torah's demand upon us to properly and meaningfully perform this mitzvah in its optimal fashion. Instead of standing aloofly outside of the mitzvah and conjecturing about its rationale, we do our best to enter into its world, feel out its contours, and emerge with fresh insight into the totality of Torah and mitzvos.

Nevertheless, while engaged in this endeavor, we must also remind ourselves that the mitzvos, emanating as they do from the infinite Divine mind, are themselves infinite; they carry inexhaustible levels of meaning and purpose.

Even with such caveats, suggesting an approach to one of the Divine commandments is no simple matter and must be approached with more than a little trepidation. I have tried to present the arguments that I believe lead to the theories proposed. My hope is that the reader will approach the material critically but with an open mind, differentiating between fact and theory, evaluating the soundness of the theory and formulating alternative ideas where necessary. May Hakadosh Baruch Hu bless our joint efforts with the fruit of insight and inspiration.

הריני מוצא לרוב טעמים פרטיים מועילים, ואומר עם זאת וחכמתו יתברך
ויתעלה מעל הכל.

I have found fine reasons for most of the commandments, yet I say: The wisdom of God is above all [human reasoning].

Rav Saadiah Gaon, HaEmunos V'HaDeios 3:2

Joy Reclaimed

CHAPTER 1

The Mitzvah
and the Questions

I t's the morning of the fifteenth of Tishrei, the first day of Sukkos, and the anticipation is palpable. As the *chazzan* approaches the end of the repetition of the *Shemoneh Esreh*, there is a buzz in the air as Lulav holders are unzipped, moist towels unwrapped, and Esrog boxes opened. The excitement is mixed with some trepidation as one person peers at his Esrog, scanning it for any imperfection that might have escaped his attention until now; another eyes his Hadassim, wondering anxiously whether the three-leaf pods are really symmetrical after all.

Admittedly, not everyone in the synagogue is Rav Levi Yitzchak of Berditchev, who would reportedly remain awake throughout the first night of Sukkos, waiting impatiently for sunrise so that he could take the Arba Minim into his hands.[1] But everyone has been looking forward to the dramatic moment during which they will fulfill the once-a-year mitzvah[2] of taking up the Arba Minim enumerated by the Torah[3]—the Esrog (citron), the Lulav (palm frond), the Hadassim (myrtle branches), and the Aravos (brook-willows).

---

1   *Zechus Yisrael: Eser Oros*, p. 86.
2   Outside of the Beis Hamikdash, the Biblical mitzvah applies only on the first day of Sukkos. In the Beis Hamikdash, it applies for all seven days of Sukkos. Today, there is a Rabbinic mitzvah to take the species throughout all the days of Sukkos, not including Shabbos, as commemoration of the Beis Hamikdash.
3   *Vayikra* 23:40.

What is the meaning, nature, and essence of this mitzvah? What is it designed to accomplish? Put differently, what effect does the Torah wish for it to have on us?

The mitzvos, in general, are designed to elevate, uplift, and, perhaps most importantly, transform us. What transformation does the mitzvah of the Arba Minim intend to catalyze within us? In what way is handling these botanical samples designed to change the way we act, think, live, and relate to God? What permanent effect is it designed to have on us?

Surveying the panorama of the Torah's mitzvos, we see that the Torah has given us mitzvos that address all parts of ourselves and all areas of life. Each mitzvah engages—and develops—a different part of our personality.[4] The human being is an immensely complicated organism, and the Torah has designed the mitzvos specifically in such a way that all aspects of ourselves are addressed and affected. Each mitzvah, aside from whatever technical act it might call for, expresses its own emotion or set of emotions; each mitzvah has its own unique nature, content, and contours. Each mitzvah brings us into a world of its own.

What, then, are the contours of this particular mitzvah? Which part, or parts, of ourselves is it designed to engage and affect? Which unique emotions does it express? What are the messages contained within it?

לו היה לי פנאי של כמה שנים, הייתי מקבל על עצמי להוכיח בשיטה פסיכולוגית-
מעשית, איך מעשי המצוות "מקדשים" את האדם...

If I had a few years' time at my disposal, I would take upon myself the task of demonstrating how the mitzvah-acts "sanctify" the human being in a psychological, practical way...

Rabbi Shlomo Wolbe[5]

---

4   "For each part of the body, and for each emotion, Hashem gave a different mitzvah" (*Midrash Tadshei* 9).

5   Private communication, published in *Journal Tiferes Yisrael* 4, p. 122.

It might come as a surprise, but anecdotal evidence suggests that some very fine Jews are troubled by this mysterious mitzvah. In one evidently true, somewhat humorous vignette, an observant lawyer, circling the *bimah* with his Arba Minim, suddenly turned and remarked to the person behind him, "If my banker were to see me now, he would never allow me credit in his bank again."[6] Although this gentleman is not alone in his feelings, the incident is probably not indicative of most people's state of mind. Still, we all can benefit from renewed exploration into this mitzvah.

For the purposes of this discussion, perhaps take a step back and pretend to be encountering the mitzvah of the Arba Minim for the first time. Would you agree that it appears somewhat bizarre?

There are numerous factors that conspire to make this mitzvah appear unusual.

First, it would seem that most, if not all, of the mitzvos that we actively perform have a seemingly rational explanation. Let's take some examples.

The strings worn on the corners of our four-cornered garments might initially appear puzzling, but are easily understood at the most basic level: they function as a reminder of the mitzvos, just as someone might tie a string around another's finger to remind him of something.[7] They are worn on four corners so that we surround ourselves with reminders of the mitzvos; in so doing, we create a space defined by allegiance to God's commandments.[8] There are, of course, infinite levels of depth and meaning to the mitzvah of tzitzis, but it seems eminently understandable even at the most basic level. Shabbos observance, at the simplest level, is testimony to our belief in the creation of the universe by the hand of God. We recite *Birkas Hamazon* after eating to express our gratitude to Hashem for sustaining us. We eat matzoh in order to recall the exodus from Egypt. We sit in a sukkah in order to commemorate God's protection of our ancestors in the desert with the Clouds of Glory.

---

6   Related in *Yedid Nefesh: Introduction to the Study of Kabbalah*, preface, p. 18.

7   See *Mishnah Berurah* 24:1, citing *Tur*.

8   See *Shulchan Aruch, Orach Chaim* 8:4.

The mitzvah of the Arba Minim, on the other hand, does not easily lend itself to straightforward explanation.

True, as the Torah itself indicates, the mitzvah is somehow connected to celebrating the ingathering of the crops and thanking Hashem for His bounty. Yet the mitzvah is still shrouded in mystery. As Rav Shamshon Raphael Hirsch points out, if the mitzvah was exclusively connected to the new crop, it would seem more intuitive to celebrate with actual crops, or with any of the seven special fruits associated with the land of Israel. Moreover, many of us today do not live a lifestyle that revolves around an agricultural cycle; are we to assume that this mitzvah holds no meaning for us at its basic level?[9]

The mitzvah of the Arba Minim is also unique in terms of how the mitzvah is performed. It would seem to be the only mitzvah that is fulfilled simply by taking something into one's hands. We do not eat it like matzoh; we do not relocate like we do with the sukkah; we don't blow or hear as we do with the shofar; we do not tie it to ourselves as we do with tefillin; we simply "take" the Arba Minim. What is the significance or associated symbolism of just taking something into our hands?

Even stranger, although one discharges his obligation by taking up the species, ideally, they are to be "shaken" or "waved" in several different directions. Moreover, all of this seemingly strange activity is conducted while we recite *Hallel*. What's going on?

Unique Details

For the halachically sensitive, there are more unusual details. All mitzvos are to be performed in an aesthetically pleasing manner; this is the concept of *hiddur mitzvah*. No other mitzvah object, though, is *disqualified* because it is not "nice-looking" enough. It is only the Esrog, as well as the other three species, that become invalidated[10] if they do not live up to the qualification of *"hadar,"* generally translated as

---

9   It is also noteworthy that unlike many other mitzvos that apply only in Eretz Yisrael, the mitzvah of the Arba Minim is applicable everywhere, even in those locales and climates in which Sukkos does not occur at the time of gathering the harvest. Clearly, then, there are dimensions to this mitzvah that are not directly dependent on the agricultural cycle.

10   See *Sukkah* 29b.

"beauty." Why is *hadar*, normally a praiseworthy addition to a mitzvah, an essential feature of this mitzvah?

Most mitzvah objects do not need to be owned by the person performing the mitzvah. One may wear borrowed tefillin, blow a borrowed shofar, or sit in a borrowed sukkah.[11] Why must one own the Arba Minim in order to discharge one's obligation with them on the first day of Sukkos?

High Stakes

The question of the meaning of the mitzvah of the Arba Minim may prove weightier than simply unraveling one particular mitzvah, important as that itself may be.

Each festival expresses a theme or concept that is focused on intensively for the duration of the festival. The point, of course, is not limited to experiencing that particular component of Divine service for a day or even a week. The experience of fully engaging with that aspect during the festival allows us to incorporate it into our long-term relationship with Torah and mitzvos. We leave each Yom Tov laden with newly discovered insights and newly acquired skills, which we then implement throughout the year. Together, all of the *Yamim Tovim* mold our personalities, at the individual and communal levels, into the nation and people the Torah wishes us to become.

The activity of "taking" the Arba Minim is certainly a central aspect of Sukkos. True, on Sukkos we move into a sukkah for the seven days of the festival. We live in a sukkah on Sukkos; but what do we *do* on Sukkos? It is our activity that will define the essence of the days.

If we do not have a grasp of what this mitzvah is all about, we are clearly missing out on at least part of the essence of Sukkos, which, in turn, means there is some central spiritual commodity that the Torah is attempting to instill into us, which we are completely missing.

---

11   Possible exceptions are the tzitzis strings (see *Orach Chaim* 11:6–7) and matzoh (see ibid., 454:4), though it is far from universally accepted that one must have ownership of either of these mitzvah items in order to fulfill those mitzvos.

Even Higher Stakes

In fact, the urgency of the need to discover the basic meaning of this mitzvah is even greater than that. To put this mitzvah in perspective, let's take a look at the concept of the *Shalosh Regalim* and the order of their cycle.

The Jewish calendar revolves around these *Shalosh Regalim*. The Mikdash in Yerushalayim is the center of our existence, the place where God dwells among us, as it were. Though we must live a normal life, each family in its own home, three times yearly we are called upon to journey to the focal point of our lives and present ourselves to "be seen" before God.

The *Shalosh Regalim* themselves form a dynamic yearly cycle. In the agricultural sense, Pesach is the time of spring, when the grain ripens; Shavuos, the time of harvesting; and Sukkos, the time of gathering in and beginning to enjoy the Divine bounty.

In a parallel spiritual sense, on Pesach we celebrate the very birth of our nationhood and connection with God; on Shavuos, we commemorate the covenant we entered into with God at Sinai; and on Sukkos, which comes at the "end of the year,"[12] we celebrate the maturing of our relationship with God, looking back and exulting in our spiritual accomplishments.

Approaching from this perspective, it becomes clear that the unique way the Torah has us spend Sukkos, aside from being definitive of Sukkos itself, illuminates for us the entirety of our yearly spiritual odyssey. As the pinnacle and summation of the spiritual year, the activity we engage in on Sukkos serves not only as the grand finale, but as the very end-goal of our efforts; it sets the overarching theme that defines the entirety of our labors. By looking ahead at the activity that stands as the ultimate step of our journey, we better understand what our journey is really all about and where we are headed.

In defining Sukkos as the time during which we are to "take up [the species] and rejoice before God, your Lord," the Torah has effectively

---

12   As it is described in *Shemos* 34:22.

said, "Labor spiritually a whole year, until you reach the point that you are ready to perform the mitzvah of the Arba Minim." It is almost as if all of our mitzvos and Divine service pulsate toward the mitzvah of the Arba Minim. If we are in the dark as to the essence of this mitzvah, we just might be missing critical understanding of the entirety of our mission in life.

If we are willing to take a step back and view this mitzvah as if for the first time, with fresh eyes, we might discover an entire world of meaning hidden just beneath the surface.

> The Jew's book of fundamental beliefs is none other than his calendar! On the wings of time, God has carved the eternal words of His live-giving Torah.
>
> *Rav Shamshon Raphael Hirsch, Collected Writings 1:1*

A Mitzvah of Instruction

It is important to realize that the mitzvos affect us not only during the few minutes that we perform them.

Just by commanding us to do a certain mitzvah, the Torah educates us and molds our character.

For example, consider the Torah's repeated exhortations to have compassion upon the less fortunate. Aside from actually requiring us to take action in this area, the Torah's emphasis on this topic teaches and instructs us about its value system and where the value of compassion figures within it.

Every mitzvah carries not only a command but also a message. Simply by instructing us to do something or to refrain from something, the Torah is molding our worldview and forming our inner world.

In fact, according to the *Maharal*,[13] this is the distinctive meaning of the word "*torah*." If the word comes from "*horaah*," which means instruction, why not simply use the word "*mitzvah*"? And if it refers to

---

13   *Drush Al Hamitzvos.*

the wisdom of the Torah, why not use the word "*chochmah*," the Hebrew word for wisdom? The *Maharal* explains that the word "*torah*" refers to a command that also educates. The rules and laws of a government, for example, do not necessarily serve as a mode of education. They may be completely utilitarian. And wisdom without commandment cannot fully shape a person. It is through commandments that the Torah seeks to mold our personalities.

Accordingly, in thinking about the meaning of the mitzvah of the Arba Minim, we need to think about what statements the Torah is making when it instructs us to engage in this activity. Which values is it imparting? To what dimensions does it seek to direct our attention? What messages are imparted to us simply by virtue of the existence of this commandment, even before we actually perform it?

כל מצוות התורה וחוקיה ניתנו ללמוד מהן מלבד פרטי מצוותן את חפץ ה' מאתנו בהנהגתנו במעשה ובמחשבה ובסידור המושכלות בכל המושג אצלנו על פני האדמה ומזה למדו חז"ל את תורת המידות אם כי לא נתייחד להם דיבור מיוחד אבל הן מעיקר כללות התורה הקדושה.

All of the mitzvos of the Torah were given for us to learn not only the details of how to carry them out, but also Hashem's will from us in our conduct in action, in thought, and in developing our conception of reality.

Chazon Ish, Collected Letters 3:185

Midrashic Interpretations

By now, the reader may be wondering: Why the need to reinvent the wheel? Are we not all familiar with the Midrashic interpretations about the symbolic meanings of the species? Do we not know, for example, that the Arba Minim represent, among other things, four different types of Jews,[14] or four important body parts?[15]

---

14   *Vayikra Rabbah* 30:12.
15   Ibid., 14.

In any Torah study, it is important to distinguish between *peshat*, the simple meaning of the text, and *derash*, a deeper and more transcendent level. *Derash*, of course, is no less a part of Torah as is *peshat*. *Derash* is not mere homiletics, but a full-fledged aspect of the Divine truths of the Torah, with rules and regulations of its own. But this does not negate the need to understand Torah at a *peshat* level. Many Rishonim such as the *Rashbam* and *Ramban* toiled to discover the *peshat*-level meaning of episodes and mitzvos throughout the Torah; they did so not to negate the *derash*, but to expose the first and most basic layer of meaning, that closest to the simple meaning of the text.

We need to ask ourselves whether the Midrash proffers these explanations as those of *peshat*, or are they to be understood in the category of *derash*?

First, there seems to be no reason to assume that the Midrash is attempting to give a *peshat* explanation. It is after all Midrash, and this is Midrash's function: providing *derash*.

More specifically, as we will soon discover, the Torah defines the mitzvah as one of rejoicing. What would be the joy involved in waving symbols to the four categories of Jews, or to the four organs? And how would all this tie directly into the seasonal joy of Sukkos? We might of course be able to answer these questions homiletically, but that would defeat the purpose of our investigation.

It seems clear, then, that the Midrash is presenting symbolic meanings at the level of *derash*.[16] This would mean that our understanding of the mitzvah cannot be based on these symbolic meanings alone. Furthermore, we might be amiss in our understanding of the Midrashic symbolisms so long as we have not discovered the *peshat*-level meaning upon which the Midrash is predicated. Developing a sound understanding of the simple meaning of this mitzvah might allow us to better understand the symbolisms given by the Midrash.[17]

---

16   The *Ramban* seems to say this in his *derashah* on *Koheles* (p. 8 in *Chazon Yoel* edition; p. 181 in *Chavel* edition); see *Chazon Yoel* n. 39.

17   We will revisit the Midrashic interpretations in chap. 8.

Deeper Understandings

There are, of course, additional approaches to the mitzvah of the Arba Minim, based on the more esoteric aspects of the Torah. Especially in our generation, Kabbalistic ideas, once accessible only to a select few, have become available to anyone who wishes to access them. Studying those works, especially works of Chassidus, which draw upon Kabbalah in explaining this mitzvah (and others), can add immeasurably to our performance of the mitzvah. At the same time though, deeper understandings of Torah must always be predicated on a deep understanding of the *peshat*, the simple level of Torah, which can be clearly grasped and internalized.

Peshat as the Baseline

Commenting on the statement that "a verse does not depart from its literal meaning,"[18] the *Maharal* writes:[19]

> This is because [the level of] peshat comes before that of der-ash. Therefore, it is necessary that the peshat, as well, be true. If only the derash were true, the Torah, Heaven forbid, would not be entirely true.
>
> Furthermore, [if only the derash were true,] it would emerge that the Torah had been given only to the select few who know the derash, and not to all of Yisrael. But the Torah is given to all of Yisrael, great and small; so the peshat, as well, must be true.

אף על פי שכל חוקי התורה גזירות הם כמו שביארנו בסוף מעילה ראוי להתבונן בהן וכל מה שאתה יכול ליתן לו טעם תן לו טעם.

Although all of the laws of the Torah are [absolute] decrees, nevertheless, it is appropriate to contemplate them; and wherever it is possible to provide a reason, one should provide a reason.

Rambam, end of Hilchos Temurah

---

18   *Shabbos* 63a.
19   *Chidushei Aggados* ad loc.

CHAPTER 2

Basic Definitions

Do we have the right to assume that there is an accessible explanation for what we are doing when we take the Arba Minim? Perhaps this mitzvah is a *chok*, an impenetrable and incomprehensible Divine command, whose meaning we are simply not privy to?

In order to respond to this question, we need to take a look at how the Torah describes this mitzvah. In doing so, we take our first, tentative steps into understanding the mitzvah of the Arba Minim.

The first and most important place to begin any investigation of a Torah mitzvah is, of course, the Torah itself. How does the Torah present the mitzvah? What is the context? What choice of words does the Torah utilize? If we are to launch any serious attempt at understanding this mitzvah, we must revisit the text of the Torah itself where the mitzvah is first introduced.

The verse presenting the mitzvah of the Arba Minim reads as follows:

וּלְקַחְתֶּם לָכֶם בַּיּוֹם הָרִאשׁוֹן פְּרִי עֵץ הָדָר כַּפֹּת תְּמָרִים וַעֲנַף עֵץ עָבֹת וְעַרְבֵי נָחַל וּשְׂמַחְתֶּם לִפְנֵי ה׳ אֱלֹקֵיכֶם שִׁבְעַת יָמִים.

And you shall take for yourselves on the first day, the product of hadar trees, branches of palm trees, the bough of a thick (or leafy) tree, and willows of the brook; and you shall rejoice before Hashem, your God, for seven days.

Vayikra 23:40

15

The Torah commands us to (a) take the species, and (b) rejoice before God for seven days. The clear implication is that the second command explains the goal of the first: Take the species and proceed to rejoice with them.

Each mitzvah-act requires a specific action. The act to be performed with tefillin is "tying;" a shofar is to be "sounded;" the activity required in a sukkah is that of "dwelling;" *k'rias Shema* is to be "spoken."

What is the essence of the mitzvah of the Arba Minim?

The essence of the mitzvah of the Arba Minim, at least as far as a simple reading of the Torah would lead us to believe, is that of "taking" the species and "rejoicing before God."

This reading of the verse is borne out by the *Rambam's* codification of this mitzvah in his list of the 613 commandments[1] as one of "rejoicing before God for seven days with the Lulav." This is echoed by numerous other Rishonim, all of whom state explicitly that the mitzvah is to utilize the species to rejoice before God.[2]

Singing Trees (I)

That our mitzvah is essentially one of rejoicing is made clear by one of the main activities the Minim are used for.

---

1   Positive mitzvah 169. See also *Sefer HaMitzvos, shoresh* 11.

2   See *Sefer HaChinuch*, 324; *Abarbanel, Vayikra* 23; *Sefer HaMaor* (end of *Pesachim*). The verse itself states that this should be done for seven days. However, the Sages explain that the seven-day requirement applies only "before God," that is, in the Mikdash. Outside of the Mikdash, only the first part of the verse, "Take for yourselves on the first day," applies. Some argue that the nature of the commandment actually varies between the one-day mitzvah that applies everywhere and the seven-day mitzvah applicable in the Mikdash. They suggest that the first involves only "taking," with "rejoicing" applying only in the Mikdash. (See, for example, glosses of Rav Yerucham Perlow to *Sefer HaMitzvos* of Rav Saadiah, vol. 3, no. 5.) However, as mentioned, the formulations of the *Rambam* and the other Rishonim indicate clearly that the nature of the mitzvah, which includes rejoicing, does not change between the one-day mitzvah outside of the Mikdash and the seven-day mitzvah within the Mikdash. Accordingly, it would seem that the simple reading of the verse is to perform this mitzvah—which includes "taking" and "rejoicing"—beginning on the first day, continuing throughout all seven days. The juxtaposition of the words "seven days" to "before God" teaches us that outside of the Mikdash, this same mitzvah is to be performed for only one day.

The actual Biblical obligation is discharged simply by having grasped the Minim in one's hands. For a more optimal fulfillment of the mitzvah, one waves them. However, this is not all; there is more that we are to do with the Minim. Each day of Sukkos, the species are held while reciting *Hallel*. At certain intervals, the species are waved.[3] What is this all about?

Hallel is an expression of the joy we feel at being servants of God. It is said only on joyous occasions. According to one opinion, the very obligation of reciting *Hallel* on the festivals is a derivative of the general commandment to rejoice on those days; it is only natural, when rejoicing over matters related to God, to express that joy by praising Him with *Hallel*.

A natural outgrowth of the mitzvah of the Arba Minim, whose very purpose and function is that of rejoicing, is utilizing them to enhance and embellish the official expression of praise and exuberance before God, that of *Hallel*.

Indeed, the Midrash explains[4] that the waving of the species during *Hallel* is derived from the Biblical verse, "Then the trees of the forest will sing joyously."[5] This verse is interpreted as referring to the Lulav, which is waved while *Hallel* is sung before God.

How exactly the species are to be utilized to enhance the recitation of *Hallel* will be better appreciated once we have developed some sense of how the species express and facilitate joy; we will revisit this topic at a later point.

Not Your Classic Joy

We have established, hopefully to the reader's satisfaction, that the very essence of the mitzvah of Lulav is that of using it to rejoice.

---

3   *Mishnah, Sukkah* 3:9.

4   *Tanchuma, Emor* 22; cited by *Tosafos, Sukkah* 37b, s.v. *be'hodu*. (See *Tosafos* and the Midrash for the specific context within which this is laid out.)

5   So inextricable are *Hallel* and the Lulav, that according to the *Rambam* and other Rishonim, the species are never waved outside of *Hallel* at all. Rather, the blessing over the species is recited, after which *Hallel* is immediately begun, with the species woven at the appropriate intervals of *Hallel*. See also *Mo'adim U'Zmanim*, 2:117.

It should be obvious that the mitzvah is not to rejoice while the species happen to be in one's hand, without there being any intrinsic connection between the species and the joy. It is clear, rather, that the species themselves are to be the facilitators of this special joy.

Perhaps, then, the Torah refers to the joy that should be experienced when performing any mitzvah?

This, too, is not feasible. The joy appropriate when performing a mitzvah is a general one, common to all mitzvos; there is no reason it should be mentioned in the context of the mitzvah of Lulav more than that of any other mitzvah. Moreover, rejoicing is given here as the very essence and definition of the mitzvah; not an emotion accompanying that act.

In defining this mitzvah as one of rejoicing, the Torah has clearly let us know that the very essence of the mitzvah is that of rejoicing and gladness. The Torah also expects us to understand just how these species are to be used to rejoice with them; otherwise, the commandment to rejoice with them would be meaningless.

In a sense, the species are tools, instruments. They are tools for generating spiritual joy. Like any tools, in order for them to be effective, it is necessary to learn how to operate them.

Certainly, if we don't know how to operate the Arba Minim, it is meaningless to speak of using them to rejoice.

Suggesting that the mitzvah of Lulav is a *chok* would negate the entire foundation of the mitzvah. If we cannot comprehend what it is that we are doing with the species, it is ludicrous to describe the mitzvah as one of "rejoicing before God."

Narrowing Down

We have viewed some facts that give us hope as to the possibility of understanding the mitzvah of Lulav. In doing so, we have discovered that the essence of this mitzvah is one of rejoicing.

What is the unique joy the Torah refers to in the context of the Arba Minim? What are we supposed to be doing with them?

The answer does not seem overly complicated. In fact, at its most basic level, the mitzvah of the Arba Minim is a rather intuitive one.

The Torah is instructing us to take these species, which are pleasing in appearance, and use them to celebrate and rejoice before God.

In the words of the *Sefer Hachinuch*, "It is known that it is the nature of these species to gladden the heart of those who see them."[6]

At the simplest and most superficial level, our verse reads exceedingly straightforward: Take these species, all of which are pleasing to the eye and to the human psyche, and by focusing on, or involving oneself with them, attain joy.

It is human nature, after all, that pleasing or attractive sights engender a sense of joy within us. As *Mishlei* tells us,[7] "The light of the eyes cheers the heart," and according to *Rashi's* interpretation, this means that pleasant sights, such as gardens of vegetation and flowing rivers have the ability to gladden the heart. The Torah, recognizing this basic phenomenon, instructs us to use it in the service of Hashem through the mitzvah of Lulav. The natural joy experienced by all humans at seeing and interacting with beautiful botanical samples is to be incorporated into a spiritual joy experienced in the service of Hashem.

Obviously, this idea needs to be embellished and unpacked, and that is what we will attempt to do in the coming chapters. But it is important to first establish this most basic, if simplistic, understanding of the mitzvah of the Arba Minim: taking items that have the natural capacity of evoking joy and using them in service of Hashem.

Back to the Reading Room

It might not be necessary to turn to *Sefer Hachinuch* or other commentaries to reach the understanding that the joy referred to by the Torah in this context is one that is evoked by the aesthetic qualities of the Arba Minim. A careful reading of the verse itself should lead to the same conclusion.

---

6   Mitzvah 324; note that *Sefer Hachinuch* goes on to explain the purpose of the joy evoked by the Arba Minim in a very specific manner; see there for details.

7   *Mishlei* 15:30.

Reading any text, and certainly the text of all texts—the Torah—requires paying attention not only to the content and precise wording it employs, but to the mood, the inflection, the melody of the text.

If you hear someone reading the verse, "And you will be for Me a kingship of priests and a holy nation,"[8] with the same inflection as, "And I will throw after you a sword avenging the revenge of the covenant,"[9] you may be sure the reader does not know what he is saying.

And no one with reading comprehension would sound the same while reading, "I did not expect to see your face; and here God has shown me your progeny!"[10] as while reading, "Hashem, why have You harmed this nation?"[11]

In reading the Torah (just as we would, *lehavdil*, in reading any text and indeed in everyday conversation), we use varying tones, inflections, and other vocal accoutrements to indicate joy or sadness, pain or excitement, fear or security, and a host of other emotions and moods.

At times, no emotion is called for. Think about reading out an address from a telephone book. It is a dry, technical matter, and is usually read in a monotone.

Let us examine the verse containing the mitzvah of Lulav.

How is it to be read in a manner that reflects its meaning and message?

It does appear to be, after all, a fairly technical verse, one that enumerates four very specific species to be used for the mitzvah. In this respect, it is similar to other verses, such as (*Vayikra* 19:6), "The Kohen shall take cedar wood, a clove, and silk of worm, and throw them into a fire."

But is it really similar?

How does the Torah refer to the various species? Note, that in the second verse we looked at, each species is called by its actual name. Yet in our verse, both the Esrog and the Hadas are not actually named, but rather referred to using descriptive terms.

---

8   *Shemos* 19:6.
9   *Vayikra* 26:33.
10   *Bereishis* 48:11.
11   *Shemos* 5:22.

In describing the Esrog, the Torah does not use this word but instead talks about "the fruit of a beautiful tree." The same is true of the Hadas: the Torah utilizes descriptive language in identifying it. Instead of calling it by name, the Torah calls our attention to its unique character.

Why does the Torah take this approach? Why not simply call them by name, as the Torah does with the cedar wood, the clove, and the silk of worm?

It seems clear that the Torah seeks, in this verse, not only to identify the necessary species, but also to inform us of the reason for the selection of each of the species.

Put differently, we need to realize that our verse is a poetic one. Instead of a prosaic enumeration of the necessary ingredients, the Torah waxes lyrical, specifically using evocative language, to allow us to penetrate to the core of the mitzvah itself.

It is not necessary to wait for the end of the verse—the part that speaks openly about "rejoicing"—to discover the flavor of this mitzvah. The Torah is quite open, from the very beginning of the verse, about the direction it is taking regarding the Arba Minim.

Merging the beginning of the verse with its end, we see the Torah commanding us to use species especially recognized for their beauty and vitality, to the end of rejoicing with them.

כשנתבונן באיזה פרשה שבתורה...ונתובנן על כל אות ותיבה שבה כמה הלכות יש בה וכן כשנחפש במדרשים ובזוה״ק ונראה כמה עניני קדושת המדות ועניני חכמה נוכל ללמוד מכל עניך נראה ברור כי מעשה אלקים המה לכלול באיזה פסוקים קצרים כמה אלפי הלכות וכמה עניני חכמה...

When we contemplate any *parashah* in the Torah...and contemplate how many halachos are contained in each word and letter; and we search in the Midrashim and Holy *Zohar* and see how many concepts of sacred character traits and wisdom are contained [in every passage of the Torah] we can see clearly that only a Divine act could place within a few short verses so many thousands of halachos and items of wisdom...

Preface of Chafetz Chaim to Likutei Halachos

Hadar

The Torah refers to the Esrog, the first specimen on the list, as the "fruit of a tree of *hadar*." The translation most often given for *hadar* is "beauty," and we will use that rendition for the time being.[12]

The Torah's reference to the Esrog as "the fruit of a tree of *hadar*" has a double meaning. The simple, primary meaning is that of identifying the species: it must be the one that is described generally as "*hadar*." The secondary meaning, though, is that the *particular specimen* being used for the mitzvah must itself possess the quality of *hadar*, or beauty. If it is flawed, then although it still belongs to the species of "fruit of a tree of beauty," it is disqualified because it itself cannot be called "beautiful."[13] Thus, "beautiful" is used not only in the sense of identifying the necessary type of tree and fruit, but also as a criterion that must be met by the actual specimen being used for the mitzvah.

Although the requirement of *hadar* is written only regarding the Esrog, the Oral Torah teaches us that this criterion applies to all four of the species.[14]

The Esrog, then—and, as explained by the Oral Torah, all of the Arba Minim—must meet the criterion of "beautiful." This is unprecedented in the Torah. What other mitzvah can only be fulfilled with an object that is beautiful?

Why this emphasis on beauty? Surely it is folly to assume that the intersection of beauty and joy in this one verse and its derivate mitzvah is coincidental. It seems much more reasonable to assume, as indeed the *Abarbanel* (*Vayikra* 23:40) does, that the very reason for the requirement of *hadar* is the joy-inducing impact it provides.

The Four Species were selected because of their natural propensity to evoke feelings of joy. It is therefore imperative that the specimens taken in fulfillment of the mitzvah be those capable of evoking such joy. It is not enough that they belong to a *species* that generally arouses joy; the specimens themselves must possess beauty.

---

12   In chapter 3, we will adjust this translation somewhat.
13   See *Sukkah* 29b.
14   *Sukkah* 31a.

It's Alive!

As we have seen, the commentators see the species as joy-inducing on account of their attractive and pleasing appearance.

We would be remiss, though, to focus solely on the beauty of the species. Precious stones, gold and silver or other commodities may also be beautiful. Yet they lack a critical joy-inducing quality: *life*.[15]

The human spirit is exhilarated and enthralled by life. Plant life speaks to and awakens the spark of life in each of us; life responds to life. And joy, of course, is inextricably bound up with a feeling of being truly alive and vibrant.

Artificial flowers have a certain beauty; they are certainly better than nothing. They may even be more perfect than real flowers. Yet as perfect as their manufacturer may fashion them, they cannot compete with authentic, real flowers. They have no soul, no life.

It is not only the pleasant appearance of the species but the life force coursing through them that gives them their unique ability to evoke a feeling of joy and gladness.

This effect of the life coursing through the species is present at a minimal level even without our conscious awareness of it. However, the more conscious an effort we make to access the part of ourselves that is aroused by life, and the more we contemplate the species and appreciate the simple life force coursing through them, the stronger the effect.

The Flower in the Room

At this point, we cannot ignore a rather obvious question. Are the Arba Minim the most beautiful plants to be found? Certainly, there are nicer looking plants out there! Why not command us to take up a bouquet of flowers? Tulips, violets, daffodils? Roses?

In the coming chapters, we will attempt to demonstrate the uniqueness of the Arba Minim. And we will revisit the flower question in a later chapter.

---

15   Obviously, being cut from the ground, the Arba Minim are no longer truly alive in the fullest sense; but they still maintain their vitality for some time. In fact, once they have lost that vitality, they are disqualified, as will be discussed at the beginning of Section 3.

Spending Time with the Species

Before addressing the unique nature and character of the Arba Minim, let's return to a basic understanding of the mitzvah, based on what we have learned thus far.

The Torah wants us to rejoice with the species. What does this entail practically?

At the level of *peshat*, it would seem that the Torah wants us to simply take the species into our hands and allow our involvement with them to evoke joy.

It is as if the Torah has said: Focus on the species. Use their presence to evoke joy. *Spend time with them.*

An Intuitive Mitzvah

At the simplest level, the picture is clear: The Torah has given us what it views as an entirely understandable and intuitive mitzvah, one of simply using the presence of the Arba Minim to evoke joy.

Of course, as is the case with most mitzvos, the general concept expressed by the written Torah takes on specific form as it is explained in the Oral Torah. Yet these specific details do not supplant the Written Torah's presentation of the basic concept of the mitzvah. The details are exactly that: details; for the essence and underlying concept of the mitzvah, we refer to the Torah's crystal-clear presentation.

Anshei Yerushalayim

The people of ancient Yerushalayim, the Talmud relates,[16] had an interesting custom:

> *A person would come to synagogue, read k'rias Shema and recite Shemoneh Esreh with the Lulav in his hand. When he would go to visit the ill or comfort the bereaved, he would have his Lulav in his hand. When he would enter the study hall, he would give it over into the hands of his son or servant (so that he could study without distraction).*

---

16   *Sukkah* 41b.

Essentially, then, the people of Yerushalayim would spend their entire day with the species. They would put them down only when they absolutely had to. Otherwise, they would be holding them at all times throughout the day.[17] As the Gemara explains, this was recounted to demonstrate how precious mitzvos were to them. The mitzvah can be discharged even by holding the species perfunctorily, for a short period of time; but the people of Yerushalayim chose to perform it in its most expansive manner.[18]

Hands On!

As we have seen, the Arba Minim are intended to evoke the natural joy brought about by the presence of pleasant-looking, vibrant plant life.

However, the Torah does not simply instruct us to spend time with them. The Torah instructs us to "take them," which the Oral Torah explains to mean that they must actually be picked up and held in one's hands.

We must ask ourselves: Why is this necessary? Why does it not suffice simply to decorate one's home with them?

The answer seems simple enough: The Torah understands that simply seeing the species is not enough. There is a level of connection that can be fostered only by physical involvement. The Species can be fully experienced, and their impact on our psyches fully had, only when taken up into our hands and handled directly.

Ultimately, the Torah wishes for us to reach a certain type of spiritual joy, but attaining that joy is facilitated by experiencing the natural joy stimulated by the species. That natural joy is best experienced when we actually get physically involved with the species.

Your Very Own

As we noted above, the mitzvah of taking the Arba Minim, at least as far as its first day is concerned, comes with an unusual requirement: One must own them in order to discharge his obligation. The species

---

17   It is reported that the Gaon of Vilna followed this custom (*Aliyos Eliyahu*, note 117).

18   In later chapters, we will revisit this passage to discover additional depth in the practice of the *Anshei Yerushalayim*.

may not be borrowed. This law is derived from the Torah's wording of the mitzvah: "Take for yourselves," which the Oral Torah explains to mean that the species must be the actual property of the person performing the mitzvah.

We noted that this is an unusual requirement that is not common to most mitzvos, if any, other than this particular mitzvah.

In light of the approach we have developed to understanding this mitzvah, perhaps we can suggest that it is the essential nature of the mitzvah of the Arba Minim that necessitates ownership. After all, the very essence of the mitzvah is utilizing the species to elicit joy. A certain element of personal connection is necessary for this to be effective. Seeing, or even handling the species, does not have enough of an impact if there is no real connection between the handler and the specimens. It is the conducting of a transaction and retaining ownership that provides this connection.[19]

From Natural Joy to Spiritual Joy

The Torah has instructed us to utilize the species to arouse joy. As we have already noted, it seems obvious that the endgoal is not simply to experience the natural joy evoked by the appearance of the species. Rather, the objective is for the natural joy to be harnessed to arouse feelings of spiritual joy having to do with God and our relationship with Him.

It would seem that the Torah expects us to have deep, if dormant, feelings of spiritual joy over our relationship with Hashem, our being part of the Chosen Nation, and over the gift of Torah and mitzvos. The physical items of the Arba Minim, by evoking a natural joy within an intense spiritual setting, have the ability to arouse, activate, and express those feelings of spiritual joy.

---

19 Homiletically, we might add that joy itself is a deeply personal matter. As we read in *Mishlei* 10:14, "The heart knows its own bitterness, and no one else can share its joy." Each person must reach his or her own personal joy in Torah and mitzvos and in relating to God. The Arba Minim, which are deployed as tools of rejoicing, must therefore be the personal property of the person using them.

The Torah understands that the natural senses, when utilized properly, can lead to spiritual states. What starts out as a natural, this-worldly joy, segues into a spiritual, transcendent joy.

לפי שהאדם מהיותו בעל חומר צריך התעוררות גדול אל הדברים, כי הטבע מבלי
מעיר יעמוד כישן.

Man, with his materialistic nature, needs great arousal to spiritual matters; without this, his psyche is as if asleep.

Sefer Hachinuch, 384

Segue

The idea that external stimuli create a climate of joy that is then channeled into a spiritual feeling is, of course, not new. The Torah commands us to "rejoice" on the festivals, which the Talmud interprets to mean that each person should use those means that bring joy to him or her. There, as well, the ultimate goal is to rejoice over spiritual matters, yet the state of joy is brought about through purely physical activities.

Still, the connection between natural joy and a more meaningful spiritual joy may require some more contemplation before it is fully appreciated.

Let us take the example of a wedding. The bride, groom, and their friends and family may dance to lively music in celebration of the occasion.

Are people not happy enough about the wedding? Why the need for music?

And if music can make you happy, does that mean that anyone can simply turn on some wedding music and be as happy as the bride or groom or their close relatives?

We might even ask further: Why is everyone dressed up? Why the need for a fancy hall, flowers, fancy cutlery? If the occasion is truly joyous, perhaps everyone, including the bride and groom, could turn up in their street clothes, get together in an auditorium, eat peanut butter and jelly sandwiches, and sit around and just "be happy."

The answer, of course, is that a wedding is cause for joy, but that joy can better be felt and expressed when there is an outside joy-inducing stimulus at hand. Of course, the stimulus on its own never could evoke the intensity of joy brought about by the occasion of the marriage.

Lively music, dress clothes, and regal surroundings are not, on their own, a source of joy. But when used to create an ambience for an independently joyous occasion, they allow the latent joy to be felt and expressed.

How do these two seemingly unrelated things fuse? How is it that the external stimulus has the ability to arouse a joy unrelated to the stimulus?

Clearly, though there are so many levels within the human organism, they are all connected. The human being is not a bunch of different facets thrown together. He (or she) is a continuum; beginning with the most basic instincts, drives and consciousness, segueing into more refined, though still corporeal, senses, continuing into the intellect and thought, and culminating in the highest spiritual awareness. There are no jumps; each level leads directly into the next. Thus, any effect on one level of the human being will necessarily impact not only the immediately adjacent levels, but the entirety of the personality.

If Sukkos is the wedding, the joyous occasion, then the Arba Minim are the music, the hall, and all of the "props" used to create the appropriate ambience for the celebration.

Sukkos Joys

To put this in general context, we need to understand what the general joy of Sukkos is all about. This is not the main topic of this book, so we will sketch broad lines.

At its simplest level, Sukkos is the culmination of the agricultural cycle. All of the *Shalosh Regalim* are built around the yearly milestones of the sprouting, harvesting, and finally ingathering of the yearly crop. Having spent the entire year preparing for, and finally reaping, the fruits of God's bounty, we rejoice before Him and express our gratitude.

Yet at a deeper level, our joy over the harvest is not a purely materialistic one. The Divine bounty, experienced specifically in the Land bequeathed to us by God, is in reality but an expression of God's providence over and special relationship with us.

At a deeper level still, Sukkos signifies the culmination of a year's work of spiritual strivings and efforts. Inasmuch as the *Shalosh Regalim* serve as the core of the Jewish calendar, Sukkos represents the end of each year's cycle of spiritual growth as well as the beginning of the next year's mission. Essentially, then, the joy of Sukkos is one of celebrating our connection with Hashem and His Torah.

It is, of course, impossible to ignore the fact of Sukkos coming directly on the heels of Rosh Hashanah and Yom Kippur, with the spiritual cleansing and reconciliation with God that they catalyze.

As the Torah makes clear, and as we recite in our prayers on Sukkos, Sukkos is the ultimate time of joy—even more so than the other two *Regalim*. Yet not only does it warrant more intense joy, the Torah has ordained that this joy be evoked and expressed in a very specific way, namely that of utilizing the Arba Minim.

The Torah wants us to rejoice over these things, and to utilize the species as a way of evoking our latent spiritual feelings of joy.

The Joy of Mitzvos

Though it is not our subject, we cannot do justice to the mitzvah of Lulav without even briefly discussing its underlying antecedent: the concept of joy in our Divine service.

In the words of the *Rambam*:[20] "The joy that one should feel at serving Hashem and fulfilling the mitzvos is a great *avodah* (service)..."

Happiness and satisfaction over our lot as members of God's nation, along with our ability to serve Hashem through Torah and mitzvos is a recurring theme throughout *Tanach* and our prayers. In the book of *Tehillim*, we read consistently of David HaMelech's joy in encountering the Creator, to Whom David refers as "God, my joy and delight."[21]

In our own prayers, we exclaim daily, "We are fortunate! How good is our lot!" After reciting *k'rias Shema* each morning, we follow up

---

20   *Hilchos Lulav* 8:15.
21   *Tehillim* 43:4.

on our proclamation of submission to God's authority with a string of adjectives indicating just how we feel about this submission. The adjectives include, but are not restricted to, true, beloved, treasured, desirable, pleasant, reasonable, good, and beautiful. Clearly, acceptance of God's authority is incomplete without an affirmation of its pleasantness and our willingness to submit.

These are only a few examples; similar sentiments permeate the entirety of our liturgy. What is clear is that taking joy—and even pleasure—in our portion in life is taken for granted as being a natural part of Torah life.

Finding the Joy

The objective and goal of the mitzvah of the Arba Minim, as we have seen, is that of evoking and expressing the spiritual joy connected to our relationship with God and Torah. We should not, however, make the mistake of thinking that only someone constantly suffused with such joy can properly fulfill this mitzvah. It is not necessary to be full of uncontrollable exuberance in order to tap into the joy of the Arba Minim. So long as even the smallest pocket of joy can be found, there is what to work with.

There are many fine Jews who, for whatever reason, feel that they have unresolved issues in their relationships with Hashem and Torah. Yet this does not preclude the possibility of finding joy in Torah and mitzvos. As human beings, we are complex. We may have mixed emotions, experiencing both positive and negative feelings toward the same subject. Even someone struggling with his or her relationship with Torah need not be afraid or ashamed to acknowledge and embrace even the smallest amount of joy he or she is able to feel.

Riding the Wave

As we noted earlier, the mitzvah of the Arba Minim includes actual physical involvement with the species.

There is another part of the mitzvah, as well. For optimal fulfillment of the mitzvah, one must not only hold the species but must also move them back and forth, as well as up and down (*Sukkah* 37b). Surprisingly, the Talmud never makes clear the source for this activity. Where does it come from?

What's more, it is not entirely clear what the purpose of this activity is. We may be used to it but imagine seeing this ritual practiced for the very first time. What is it all about?

It would seem that the theme of waving the species is the same as that of the mitzvah itself: experiencing or expressing joy.[22] The movement of the species, which to begin with are joy-evoking items, adds another dimension of joy to the experience.

Some suggest that the very source for this added activity is the Torah's command to "rejoice" with the species.[23] The Sages understood that full rejoicing is to be had, or expressed, only through movement. An individual actively expressing joy may clap his hands, jump up and down, or even dance; he certainly does not stand still. If the Torah commands us to take the species and "rejoice" with them, what it really is asking of us is to perform movements expressing joy.

The Art of Expression

If indeed the waving and shaking of the species is for the sake of expressing joy, we may have discovered an additional aspect of the mitzvah.

If until now we had assumed that the objective and essence of the mitzvah is that of using species to *evoke* joy, we now know that the mitzvah includes not only *evoking* feelings of joy to be passively experienced, but also actively *expressing* those feelings of joy.

The species thus serve a dual function: they both evoke joy as well as express it.

As we have already established, the species do not evoke spiritual joy per se; rather, they evoke natural joy that in turn arouses a corresponding spiritual joy.

What type of joy do we express by waving the species? Clearly, we are expressing the spiritual joy that was the ultimate goal of the natural joy.

---

22 See also *Meiri* to *Sukkah* 38b, who states this with regard to shaking the species during *Hallel*.
23 Rav Leib Mintzberg, *Ben Melech: Sukkos*, p. 62; Rav Menachem Schlanger, *Mishnas Torah, Emor*, p. 773.

In summary, the Minim are used to evoke feelings of natural joy, which in turn arouse feelings of spiritual joy. Simultaneously, the species themselves are utilized to express those feelings of spiritual joy.

Singing Trees (2)

As we saw in an earlier chapter, a primary activity for which we utilize the Minim is that of reciting *Hallel*. What is this all about?

When people converse animatedly, they may punctuate and emphasize their words with hand motions and gesticulations. The more animated the conversation, and the more passionate the orator, the more animated the gesticulations. Body movements allow us to express thoughts and feelings in ways, and with an intensity, that go beyond the spoken word.

When people really want to communicate passionately, they utilize props. Your schoolteacher may have gestured with a piece of chalk or a marker; fans or patriotic citizens wave flags or other paraphernalia; victorious military men bear aloft their weapons to celebrate victory. All use physical items to better express and make tangible their sentiments.

Holding something in your hands makes what you're saying real. You're not only saying something, not only accentuating it with body language, but taking something else into your hands to proclaim it. It's the ultimate way of expressing what's in your heart.

The Sages understood that at their most basic level, the Arba Minim are to be used as physical props punctuating and enhancing our expressions of joy and praise before God.[24]

The species evoke a natural joy that is then harnessed to express the spiritual joy voiced through saying *Hallel*. Reciting *Hallel* while holding and waving joy-inducing specimens allows for a deeper and more robust expression of joy and praise.[25]

---

24   One of the parts of *Hallel* during which we wave the species is upon reciting the verse, "O Hashem, please save [us]!" This seems somewhat counterintuitive if the purpose of waving is to express joy. It would appear that waving at that point is associated with the protection attained by waving the species, which we deal with briefly in chapter 8.

25   The *Ramban* (glosses to *Sefer HaMitzvos*, *Shoresh* 1) suggests that reciting *Hallel* with the Lulav on Sukkos may be a Biblical obligation. Rav Yitzchak Ze'ev Soloveitchik, the Brisker Rav, suggests in his work on the Torah that according to the *Ramban*, when the Torah

Is This All?

We have discovered that at its most basic level, the essence of the mitzvah of the species is utilizing the natural joy they evoke to arouse a deeper, more spiritual joy.

Some might find this difficult to accept. It seems too trivial to lie at the core of a Divine commandment.

Besides, what great joy do these species evoke, after all? Any feelings of joy stimulated by the sight of the Arba Minim seems negligible, at best.

Is the effect of these species so profound that it can explain a Biblical commandment? Why is the Torah making such a big deal out of these species?

These are legitimate questions that deserve a serious and thoughtful response.

The Mitzvah-Acts

To answer these questions, we will need to take a step back and take a look at the entire category of mitzvos *maasiyos*, those mitzvos that involve physical actions. What is the purpose of these mitzvos, and why must physical items and actions be involved?

Why does the Torah ordain that we wear tzitzis in order to remember the mitzvos and keep ourselves from straying after the heart and eyes? Can these things not be accomplished without strings attached to our clothing?

Why does the Torah require a Jewish man to wear boxes containing core passages of the Torah? Why not instead simply require us to constantly contemplate these passages?

Why must we eat matzoh in order to remember the Exodus? Surely it is possible to reminisce about that event without eating unleavened bread?

The same can be asked concerning blowing the shofar and sitting in the Sukkah. And considering the Rabbinic mitzvos, kindling Chanukah lights and reading the *Megillah* on Purim as well.

---

instructs us to "rejoice" before Hashem with the Arba Minim, this means to use them to recite *Hallel*, which is an expression of joy.

Consistently, the Torah requires us to perform physical acts to inculcate certain memories, beliefs, and awareness within ourselves. Why so?

The Torah recognizes that though our intellect may respond to intellectual stimulation, we are also partly physical beings, and our physical and material sides need to be reached as well. The way to train our physical sides into proper living and understanding is through physical actions and even the usage of props.

The significance of the impact physical stimuli can have on our consciousness is a concept heavily stressed by the *Sefer Hachinuch* who sees the basis of all physical mitzvos as the effect these acts have on our psyches, including our subconscious minds.[26] The *Sefer Hachinuch* explains at length that actions have a profound, if subtle, effect on our personalities.

In our times, this concept is better understandable than perhaps ever before. So much is known about the subconscious mind and the profound effects of even unnoticed stimuli. Advertising capitalizes on man's easy impressionable nature in myriad ways. What was a revelation in the early days of psychological research is now common knowledge. Today, it is commonly understood that our subconscious processes affect us much more profoundly than our conscious thoughts. The power of association, for example, is one that operates entirely on a subconscious level, and dictates so many of our reactions to the things that happen in our lives.

The Torah understands that the path to our subconscious mind is through the actions as well as stimuli that affect it. The simple act of gazing at the strings of the tzitzis affects us in a way that simply thinking about their message never could. Tying the tefillin boxes onto our bodies solidifies the realities contained in their passages in such a way that just thinking about them never could.

Eating matzoh with the conscious awareness that we took matzoh with us as we left Mitzrayim brings us back to the moment of the Exodus in a way that mere reminiscing is incapable of.

---

26   Mitzvos 16, 95, 286, 388, 489.

Spending a week in a Sukkah as a way of remembering the Clouds of Glory gives a realness to our memories of those events that cannot be accomplished simply by thinking about them. And the same for all of the physical mitzvos.

The secret of the physical mitzvah-acts is the sending of subconscious messages to the deepest recesses of our psyches.

Appreciating the Subtlety of the Psyche

In the previous chapter we noted that the primary function of the physical mitzvah-acts is that of affecting the psyche. This, of course, would mean that the Torah presupposes that the psyche of the human being is susceptible to being profoundly affected by even the most innocuous of actions; that we are, simply put, highly sensitive to external stimuli.

Perhaps this is the place to investigate the Torah's attitude toward such sensitivity. Is it even true that the Torah expects, encourages, or condones such sensitivity? After all, we might imagine that a fully developed Torah personality will have transcended the sensitivity toward petty physical matters.

Is our sense of aesthetics to be overcome or to be cultivated?

There may, of course, be multiple perspectives on this issue, but we will explore one particular approach.

Rav Yosef Leib Bloch, in his classic *Shiurei Daas*,[27] discusses an incident cited by the Talmud:

> *Rabbi Akiva saw a non-Jewish woman who was exceedingly beautiful. Upon seeing her, he spat, laughed, and wept. He spat at the thought that she, with all her beauty, had issued from "a putrid drop." He laughed because he foresaw that she would convert, and he would marry her. He wept at the thought that such beauty was destined to "decompose in the earth."*

Rav Bloch notes that all of these reactions were spontaneous and immediate. Rabbi Akiva, perhaps the greatest of all our sages, was

---

27   Vol. 1, essay on *Korbanos*.

not impervious or indifferent to the sight of unusual beauty. To the contrary, he was deeply affected by it. In fact, so sensitive was he that he was affected on multiple, seemingly contradictory fronts. This incident demonstrates, says Rav Bloch, the fact that the greater a person, the more powerful and more vivid all of his natural senses become, and the more sensitive he is to the slightest stimulus.[28]

Concerning those who remain unmoved by the marvels of creation, the Navi says (*Yeshayah* 5:12): "At the handiwork of God they do not gaze…" *Rashi*, citing the Midrash, explains: "They do not praise God, morning and evening, with the blessings concerning the rising and setting of the sun." These blessings were instituted with the assumption that a normal Jew will be so affected by the events of sunrise and sunset, that he will be moved to recite a special blessing taking note of them.

We need look no further than the book of *Tehillim*, where we consistently encounter the exquisite sensitivity of David HaMelech toward the marvels of creation.

The *Rambam* famously writes that the commandment to love God is fulfilled by taking note of the marvels of creation.[29] This, of course, presupposes some level of sensitivity to beauty and order. Can a person with no aesthetic sense at all grow to appreciate God's handiwork?

Journey to the Depths of the Psyche

If understanding the objective of the hands-on mitzvos in light of the effect they have on our psyche seems shallow to us, we might do well to investigate whether that perception may stem from a shallow grasp of what is going on within our own selves.

The human psyche is a bottomless reservoir of emotions, feelings, associations, memories, and impressions. We are actively aware of only the most superficial levels of our minds. As we have already noted, and

---

28   It is interesting to note that Rabbi Akiva's sensitivity comes through in other incidents as well. In *Chullin* 127a, Rabbi Akiva reaches the verse in *Tehillim* stating "How many are Your creations, O God," which leads him to expound on the variety and multiplicity of God's creatures. And it was Rabbi Akiva whose "eyes would drip tears" when he would read *Shir Hashirim*, "since he knew to what depths it reaches" (*Zohar, Bereishis* 98b).

29   *Yesodei HaTorah* 2:1.

as is well-known, much of our personalities, decisions, and outlooks are formed at a subconscious level. And we can never know the extent of the effects that various stimuli have on our subconscious mind.

The more an individual is attuned to his or her deeper levels of awareness, the more they are able to appreciate the inestimable power of even the simplest acts on the psyche. Of course, mitzvos, when performed as such, are not simple acts. The very fact that they are performed with reverence—after internal preparation and with the proper intent, along with various accompanying feelings—greatly intensifies the imprint they make upon us.

In fact, it could be suggested that part of our duty to generate a more robust fulfillment of the mitzvos is to further develop our awareness of what goes on inside of us. For the more we are attuned to the depths of our psyches, the greater our ability to facilitate an even deeper impression through the very same acts. By focusing on those elements that are to make an impression upon ourselves, we greatly multiply the potency of those impressions.

Impact

Returning to our mitzvah, the Torah understands the specific impact the species can have on the psyche. Properly utilized, the species have the ability to stimulate and evoke latent feelings of spiritual joy.

Though this impact is always present at some level, it can be increased when we know what to look for and how to use these stimuli consciously. Focusing and meditating upon the beauty and vitality of the species intensifies their ability to evoke feelings of natural, and subsequently spiritual, joy.

The mitzvah of tefillin cannot be performed without an arm; and one cannot fulfill the mitzvah of eating matzoh without a mouth.

Which part of the human organism is used to fulfill the mitzvah of the Arba Minim?

Practically, of course, we use our hands to fulfill this mitzvah. But inasmuch as the essence of the mitzvah is that of evoking joy, the instrument needed to fulfill it is the aesthetic sense, the part of us that thrills to life, beauty, and vibrancy. A deeper fulfillment of the mitzvah may require the inner work of locating and cultivating that part of our psyche that relates to and thrills to the joy of nature, beauty, and vitality.

Although we have focused on the joy-inducing impact of the Arba Minim, we have done so in an extremely general manner. Much work is still ahead of us before we can understand the specific and nuanced effect the Torah may wish for them to have on us.

CHAPTER 3

Getting Specific

Having established, based on the implicit message of the Torah made explicit by the Rishonim, that the basis of the mitzvah of the Arba Minim is utilizing the species' naturally gladdening appearance to facilitate rejoicing before God, we allow ourselves the following fairly obvious questions.

As we have previously noted, the Torah commands us to rejoice on all festivals, and to rejoice on Sukkos with the Arba Minim. When it comes to the general commandment of rejoicing, one fulfills the mitzvah through rejoicing with whatever means one finds appropriate. The Talmud prescribes wine for men, fine clothing for women, and nuts and roasted grain for children;[1] yet halachic authorities explain that these are but examples, and one is obligated to find whatever brings joy to him or her and to utilize whatever it may be to rejoice.[2]

With Sukkos, however, the Torah has gone a step beyond that: it has commanded us to rejoice in a very specific manner, by utilizing botanical samples to rejoice before God. This requires some explanation. Why the specific prescription, beyond the general mitzvah to rejoice?

Why, furthermore, are multiple species necessary? Why not command us to take up one attractive, joy-inducing species?

---

1   *Pesachim* 109a.

2   See, for example, *Shaagas Aryeh* 65.

And if, for some reason, the Torah wills us to take Arba Minim, why specifically *these* Arba Minim? Why not simply command us to select any Arba Minim that we find pleasing, and to rejoice with them? What is unique about each of the Arba Minim?

Why does the Torah feel the need to involve itself in a seemingly technical aspect of the mitzvah, namely, which species to utilize in rejoicing before Hashem?

Why is the Torah micro-managing the way we arrive at a state of joy?

To get a sense of just how jarring this commandment is when viewed objectively, let us look at the general commandment "to rejoice on the festivals" as a metaphor. Imagine if the Torah were to command us, in that context: "Thou shalt rejoice on each of your festivals with a glass of Pinot Gris, two steaks with garlic, alfalfa sprouts, and potatoes roasted for thirty-eight minutes at a temperature of 320°F." This would be absurd. Surely, if the objective is attaining a spirit of joy, prescribing a detailed and objective menu is not only unnecessary but counterproductive. What if I dislike Pinot Gris, preferring instead Cabernet Sauvignon? And what if I dislike wine altogether, preferring instead a cold glass of seltzer? And if I prefer turkey, must I force myself to "rejoice" with a steak?[3]

Yet upon reflection, it seems as if this is precisely what the Torah has done within the parallel mitzvah of rejoicing with the Arba Minim. What is this all about?

These are, of course, audacious questions, and there are those who, perhaps justifiably, would recoil from them. The Torah is, after all, filled with many cryptic and mystifying details and nuances, and it is generally accepted that some things are simply beyond our provenance. Why should the species be any different?

Why should we be surprised at discovering—even within this basically intuitive mitzvah, one of utilizing aesthetically pleasing nature to facilitate spiritual joy—an impenetrable nuance?

---

3   The Torah commands us to eat the *Korban Pesach* on the night of the fifteenth of Nissan in a very specific and prescribed manner. However, the Torah never indicates that that mitzvah has anything to do with rejoicing. It is an independent mitzvah with its own guidelines.

We may counter these objections by recalling that, as we have already pointed out, the mitzvah of the Arba Minim is clearly a mitzvah designed to impact the human psyche. It thus seems more legitimate to assume, or at least hope, that there is meaningful content to be discovered within its nuances and guidelines—content that aids us in achieving the objectives of the mitzvah and without which we may be somewhat impaired in achieving those objectives.

Four Species, Four Flavors

The questions presented above naturally seem to point us toward an understanding and assumption that, although the feature common to all Arba Minim is that of their naturally pleasing appearance, *each is pleasing in its own unique manner.*

If, as the *Sefer Hachinuch* and others tell us, the Arba Minim naturally gladden the heart, it is apparent that *each one of the species "gladdens the heart" in its own way.*

Each evokes—and, by extension, expresses—a unique form, or flavor, of joy.

The Torah, after all, has seen fit to instruct us not only on the general need to utilize pleasing species to facilitate joy, but also on which species to use. It seems eminently reasonable to assume that the Torah asks us for four very specific forms of joy, and that the species selected by the Torah are those designed specifically to evoke those specific forms of joy.[4]

The main import of this insight becomes clear when we try taking it to the next step. As we have noted earlier, the objective of this mitzvah is not simply evoking and expressing natural joy, but allowing the natural joy to arouse, and possibly to express, spiritual joy. If we are correct in assuming that the Arba Minim are designed to evoke four distinct types of natural joy, this would mean that they are then to arouse four distinct forms of spiritual joy.

---

4   The general idea that each species carries its own unique characteristic is stated clearly by the *Rambam, Moreh Nevuchim* 3:43; *Ralbag*; and *Abarbanel*, though none take the particular approach that we attempt to develop below.

If we are on the right track, the Torah has in essence prescribed a "bouquet" specially designed to evoke the very particular and specific forms of joy it deems important and necessary.

In fact, the example of a bouquet might prove instructive. Anyone who knows anything about flowers knows that one cannot simply slap together a bunch of flowers and call them a bouquet. The flowers must complement each other, fit each other. They must "go together."

Each flower, with its unique coloring, shape, and character, has a unique impact upon the psyche, and if the various effects are not coordinated, the effect is not uplifting or meaningful but rather jarring.

Answering the question of "why these four specific species" would necessitate an attempt at ascertaining precisely which form of joy is evoked by each species. Were we to figure this out, we would then be able to reason that these forms of joy are what the Torah has in mind for us in the context of Sukkos. We could then attempt to discern why these specific forms of joy are important.

Revving Up for the Search

We are now prepared to take on the task of searching for the particular form of natural joy to be evoked by each species, and in turn, what unique form of spiritual joy is to be aroused by each form of natural joy.

What form should our search take?

We could, perhaps, ponder the symbolism of each species. We could scour the Torah for references to each one and attempt to put together an index of representation, then attempt to couple those symbols with various forms of joy.

Yet one senses that such an approach ignores the viscerally experiential nature of this mitzvah. The mitzvah at its simplest, initial level speaks not to the mind or soul but to the psyche. It is addressed to the aesthetic sense. The joy that it most immediately evokes is a natural joy, one that requires no cerebration or contemplation. To attribute each species' unique form of joy to the intellectual concept that it "symbolizes" would be to pull the rug out from under the basis of the entire mitzvah.

If the basic joy common to all of the species is a natural, intuitive one, the unique form of joy specific to each must also, it would seem, be a natural, intuitive form of joy.

This being the case, our quest for uncovering the unique properties of each species should be an *experiential* one. We need do nothing more than engage the species—gaze at them or their pictures, or, at the very least, visualize them—and take notice of what effect, however subtle, each has upon us.

More specifically, we might compare the Arba Minim and the effect they have upon us with other types of plants or fruit; using other species as a foil can help us sharpen our awareness of the species' unique effect.

The Torah, after all, was given to us as human beings, to have an effect on our human psyches.

Searching for the exact effect each of the Arba Minim has on our psyche necessitates delving deeply into the recesses of our minds and sensitizing ourselves to what goes on in our psyche. In a way, in order to get to the bottom of this mitzvah we would need to put our psyche under a microscope and analyze it, discovering just exactly how it responds to various stimuli.

המפרש הכי מובחר על התורה הוא האדם בעצמו.

The best commentary on the Torah is the human being himself.

Rav Yerucham Levovitz, cited in Alei Shur II, p. 16

Divine Clues

There is, however, another possible set of clues that can lead us on our search. These are the words used by the Torah to identify the Arba Minim. If we are to launch any serious attempt at understanding this mitzvah, we must revisit the text of the Torah itself where the mitzvah is first introduced.

Listening to the Music

Before we investigate further, let us return to the beginning of our verse in an attempt to actually "hear" what it has to say.

As we have already noted, at least regarding the Hadas and Esrog, the Torah does not identify these species by name. Instead, the Torah uses code names: "the fruit of a beautiful tree," and, "the frond of a plaited tree." This is highly unusual, if not absolutely unprecedented. Certainly, there are instances in which the Torah will mention an item without giving its details, such as a sukkah. However, the Torah has referred to the hut as a sukkah, which is the most accurate and specific way of referring to it. The Torah speaks of a "day of sound-making" without referring to the instrument to be used—a shofar. In that case, though, the Torah avoids making explicit reference to the shofar altogether. In our case, on the other hand, the Torah is clearly referring to something specific, but refuses to name it. Why so? Why can the Torah not simply state "take an Esrog/Hadas?" Why the secrecy?

It would seem that the point is precisely that the Torah is communicating to us that it is not interested in the Esrog per se. It is interested in "the fruit of a *hadar* tree." It is not inherently interested in a Hadas per se; it is interested in "a frond of a plaited tree." As it happens, the ultimate *pri eitz hadar* is an Esrog, and the only plant answering to the specifications of *anaf eitz avos* is a Hadas. It is not their inherent identity but their qualifications that are desired, and the Torah makes this eminently clear by avoiding even mentioning them by name.

If this is the case, it seems clear that the Torah itself is showcasing the unique properties of each of the Minim and why it was selected for this mitzvah.[5]

If our theory—that each species evokes a specific type of joy—is correct, and our intuition—that the Torah identifies that which makes each species unique and that led to its selection—can be trusted, then we may assume that the Torah is telling us what it is about each species

---

5   See the *Ralbag* who makes this point regarding the Lulav, as well as *sefer Ben Melech*, p. 68, who propounds this general idea with regard to all four of the species.

that evokes a unique form of joy. The Torah is essentially alluding to the unique form of joy evoked by each species.

If our postulates are correct, these two methods—that of probing the unique effect had by the species upon our psyches, as well as a careful reading of the Torah's description of the species—should yield the same conclusions. The Torah's references should hit on those characteristics that we find to be outstanding in each species.

Staying Grounded

There is another advantage to using the two guidelines of human experience and the precise wording of the mitzvah.

Reading the verse containing the mitzvah of the Arba Minim, one gets the impression that the mitzvah is self-explanatory, with no need to search elsewhere to decipher its basic meaning. If nothing compels us to look far afield, we are on much safer ground in searching for meaning innate to this very verse itself. The further afield we go, the more we risk drowning in creative speculation. Keeping close to home can keep us grounded.

CHAPTER 4

The Ultimate Bouquet

Two Groups of Two

Although the Torah commands us to take Arba Minim, a closer reading might lead us to conclude that there are actually two pairs of species. The cantillation (*trop*) of the verse clearly draws a demarcation between the first two, Esrog and Lulav, and the second group of two, the Hadassim and Aravos. We will follow this lead and attempt to establish the relationship between the two members of each duo. We therefore begin our search with an investigation of the Esrog-Lulav duo.

Part 1: Esrog and Lulav

SEGMENT 1: THE FRUIT OF A *HADAR* TREE

Hadar: What Does It Really Mean?

The Torah calls the Esrog *pri eitz hadar*, the fruit of a tree of *hadar* (beauty).

As we have already suggested, the Torah is making it clear that it is not the Esrog per se that it is interested in, rather its being "the fruit of a *hadar* tree." Accordingly, if we are to understand at all why the Torah selected this fruit, we need to properly understand the meaning and significance of *hadar*.

Now we must ask a pivotal question: What does *hadar* actually mean?

We have followed conventional knowledge, as well as most traditional translations of the Torah that I have come across, in rendering *hadar* as "beautiful." And indeed, the words of the Rishonim seem to bear this translation out.

The difficulty is that even a cursory perusal of the word's usage throughout the rest of the Torah, as well as the *Neviim*, shows that the word *hadar* means something else.

Consistently, throughout Torah, *Neviim,* and *Kesuvim,* the term *hadar* means something closer to majesty, grandeur, glory, or honor. Consider, for example, the following verse (*Shemos* 33:3): "Do not display *hadar* to a pauper in his litigation." As all commentaries explain, the verse means to say, "Do not *honor* the pauper by ruling in his favor even though the law is against him." Beauty, of course, plays no role in that context.

Similarly, the Torah states, "Show *hadar* to the elder."[1] Does the Torah mean to place a beautiful wreath of flowers upon the elder's hoary head? As *Rashi* explains, *hadar* means honor. "Show *honor* to the elder."

"Prostrate before God with *hadar* of sanctity."[2] As the *Radak* explains there, *hadar* means honor. The Psalmist says, in effect, "Display honor toward God's sanctity."

A Beauty of Grandeur

It seems clear that *hadar*, in its most original and basic usage, means grandeur.

Thus, if we were to translate our verse in a way that is consonant with the usage of the term *hadar* in the rest of the Torah and *Tanach,* our verse would read, "Take for yourselves the fruit of a majestic tree," or, "regal tree."

At the same time, as we have seen, the Rishonim make it clear that *hadar* in our context is connected to beauty.

There is, of course, overlap between the concepts of beauty and honor. While not all beauty is associated with grandeur, some forms of it are. There is a beauty that expresses and reflects honor, grandness.

---

1   *Vayikra* 19:32.
2   *Tehillim* 29:2.

Apparently, *hadar* in the context of Esrog does indeed connote beauty, but a very specific flavor of beauty: the beauty of glory, majesty, and honor.

The Torah sees the beauty of the Esrog as that type of beauty that conveys grandeur. Contemplating the appearance of the Esrog, we may conclude that this particular fruit, aside from being generally pleasing to the eye, has a regal bearing; it stands straight up with pride; and its "crown," in the form of the stem known as the *pittam*, completes its kingly appearance.

Esrogim come in many different forms, and not all would be described as grand or majestic. But in a general sense, the Esrog is one of the most beautiful and grand fruits.

The Joy of Grandeur

As the Rishonim point out in the general context of the Arba Minim, beauty evokes joy. Yet there are different kinds of beauty, and each form of beauty evokes a different shade of joy. What kind of joy is the *pri eitz hadar* designed to evoke?

If we are correct in identifying the unique beauty of the *pri eitz hadar* as one of grandeur and majesty, then the joy evoked by this fruit is a type of joy borne by reflecting on something grand and lofty.

Grandeur, nobility, majesty—all of these have the ability to put us into an uplifted frame of mind. This, then, is the type of natural, aesthetic joy evoked by the Esrog.[3]

Hadras Kodesh

Having tentatively established the unique nature of the joy fostered by the Esrog, let us step back and focus on the significance of this insight.

As we discussed in chapter 2, the Torah instructs us to utilize the natural forms of joy associated with the naturally pleasing appearances of

---

3   If talk about the grandeur and splendor of the Esrog seems like overkill, imagine an Esrog blown up to ten thousand times its size. A humongous apple or peach would be interesting, but not awe-inspiring; a humongous Esrog would basically be an alp. To get a sense of this, hold an Esrog directly in front of your face, mentally "shrink" yourself and focus on the Esrog to the exclusion of all else.

the species, to awaken and evoke the spiritual joy of being God's people and having a relationship with Him.

Clearly, though, as we noted in chapter 3, it is not enough for the Torah that we experience a general sense of joy; the Torah wishes for us to experience four distinct forms of natural joy, ultimately resulting in the arousal of four distinct forms of sacred joy.

Assuming we have correctly identified the natural joy, catalyzed by involvement with the *pri eitz hadar* as the joy of loftiness and greatness, we must ask ourselves: what unique form of sacred joy is this natural joy to arouse?

It seems reasonable to posit that the function of the *pri eitz hadar* is to awaken, then express, feelings of joy at the opportunity afforded by our relationship with God to attain greatness and stateliness. The Torah defines the Jewish People as a kingdom of great people and speaks repeatedly of our uplifted status. Torah in general is that which gives us the ability to transcend, to ennoble ourselves. Perhaps, then, the Esrog, along with the natural uplifted type of joy it evokes, is designed to evoke the spiritual joy felt when one focuses on the elevation and transcendence afforded by the Torah and our relationship with Hashem.

Going further, perhaps the Esrog evokes the joy felt at standing in the presence of our Creator, the ultimate source of all grandeur, beauty, and majesty.

Of course, these two areas are related. The nobility afforded to us through Torah life is inseparable from the ultimate majesty and *hadar* of God Himself. The Torah bestows upon us a lifestyle of loftiness and transcendence because it is the revealed will of the ultimate source of the very concepts of grandeur and majesty. Torah teaches us how to become more Godly and brings us closer to God's own "nature." The joy felt at being in God's presence and the joy felt over our own attainment of Godliness are inextricably bound up with each other.

In the *berachah* of *Emes Veyatziv*, recited daily, we affirm that the fact of God being our personal God is, among other adjectives, "awesome, formidable…and beautiful." The Esrog allows us to directly experience these qualities in a most tangible and hands-on way. And concerning human beings, we read in *Tehillim*, "What is man that You remember him, and son of man that you consider him? Yet You have made him a little less than the angels, and with glory and *hadar* have You crowned him."[4]

Hadar is clearly a central concept in Torah, and the Esrog installs this quality in the Jewish psyche.

הוזהרנו בזה לזכור את הש״י בכל עת. וחייב האדם להשתדל לקנות לנפשו תמיד ההנהגות המחויבות מן הזכירה, כמו היראה והצניעות וקישוט המחשבות וטכסיס המדות. כי זרע הקודש ישיגו כל הנהגה נאוה והמעטירה בעליה מזכירת השם ית׳.

The Torah exhorts us not to forget God but to be aware of Him at all times. And this, in turn, requires us to strive for those behaviors that stem from awareness of God's existence, such as awe, modesty, adornment of one's thoughts, and perfection of character traits. For a Jew can achieve every behavior that beautifies and crowns its owner—through thinking about God's existence.

Shaarei Teshuvah 3:27, paraphrased

Bottom Up

In chapter 2, we suggested that the Torah instructs us to use physical items to arouse natural joy, which in turn is to translate into spiritual joy. Having possibly discovered one of the specific forms of joy the Torah wishes us to experience, we can revisit that idea in greater detail.

Why does the Torah not simply instruct us to focus mentally on the greatness and majesty of God, and on our great fortune in being allowed to serve and relate to Him? Why the necessity of the interim step of focusing on the low-scale grandeur and beauty of the *pri eitz hadar* as a way of evoking a natural joy?

Working off the approach we have developed so far, we can apply the idea we looked at there in a more specific sense to the species of *pri eitz hadar.*

---

4   *Tehillim* 8:5–6.

Utilizing the *pri eitz hadar* in the context of arousing spiritual joy creates a more authentic and more tangible sense of joy at God's greatness and majesty and our own attainment of Godliness.

Pondering this question can lead us to an insight that is perhaps the underlying secret of the mitzvah of the Arba Minim.

Once again, we attempt to remain consistent with our general approach throughout our search. We are working with experiential matters. Rather than over-think the issue, it makes sense to approach it experientially.

Try to conjure up a sense of joy at our opportunity to serve our Creator whose majesty, greatness, and beauty are unparalleled. Then meditate on the appearance of the Esrog (if you don't have one in front of you), tap into its beauty and grandeur. Make an attempt to connect the natural feelings of joy evoked by the *pri eitz hadar* with the spiritual joy of our said connection with the living God.

What differences might we notice?

As human beings, we incorporate various levels of personality. We have a spiritual level, an intellectual level, and natural physical levels.

Focusing on direct catalysts of spiritual joy can indeed arouse a feeling of spiritual joy, but that feeling can be detached and remote from our more natural and primal selves. Our *souls* may be joyous, but the rest of our being might not appreciate that joy.

When we focus on catalysts of natural joy within a context of spirituality and connection to our Creator, the spiritual joy evoked by this experience is *more authentic* than when we attempt to jump straight to that spiritual joy. Having been stimulated by a natural experience, it is a bottom-up, grassroots type of joy, one connected to our most basic levels of existence.

Two-Way Street

Having noted the added authenticity and tangibility of a joy brought on through natural means, let us look at an additional advantage to this method of accessing joy.

One of the natural senses with which we are endowed is that of association. Our feelings toward people, seasons, places, and other parts of life are colored by the experiences they remind us of and that which we associate them with. Every experience we have echoes through the corridors of our lives in ways we may not even be aware of.

When our sense of natural joy at beauty and grandeur, evoked by natural stimuli, is used to evoke feelings of spiritual joy at our standing before the grandeur of our Creator, two things can be expected to occur within our psyches:

First, as a result of this experience, any interaction with God—our prayer, mitzvos, and so on—will from now on automatically conjure up association with the freshness, vitality, beauty, and regality of the *pri eitz hadar*.

Second, and conversely, once the foundation has been laid for associating natural beauty and grandeur with joyous reverence before God, any encounter with natural beauty and grandeur will automatically be associated with God, our relationship with Him, and the beauty and grandeur felt in our own Divine service.

In short, our encounter with the *pri eitz hadar*, if conducted properly, has the potential to transform the way we relate to God, to earthly grandeur, and the relationship between them.

It is perhaps necessary to once again reiterate that the issue is not what the *pri eitz hadar* symbolizes or represents, rather what it is supposed to *evoke* in the human psyche. This mitzvah is about what is experienced at the most basic level, not what is thought about.

At a most basic and subconscious level, all of this will take place automatically. Obviously, though, the more one focuses on the *hadar* quality, the more of an impact it will make on the psyche.

Impact!

The mitzvah of the Arba Minim is essentially a seven-day mitzvah. In practice, this mitzvah can only be fulfilled to its fullest in the Mikdash; outside of the Mikdash it can be fulfilled only on the first day of Sukkos. Today, as a way of remembering the Mikdash, we observe the mitzvah on a Rabbinic level for the rest of Sukkos as well.

Thinking about the optimal, seven-day observance of the mitzvah, we can imagine the effect of spending an entire seven days—a full week—encountering and waving the *pri eitz hadar* in the Mikdash, with awareness of and focus on God's grandeur. This would leave an indelible impact on the psyche, using the power of association, associating the *hadar* of the Esrog with God and His Mitzvos.

The *Hadar* Factor

We have examined the unique properties of the *pri eitz hadar* and formulated a theory of the specific type of joy it is designed to evoke. Before we turn to the next of the species, we should take note of the commonality that all four of the species share with each other.

Although it is only in conjunction with the *pri eitz hadar* that the concept of *hadar* is invoked, halachah requires that all four of the species measure up to a standard of *hadar*.[5] The Sages deduced from the grouping of all Arba Minim together that they are all equal to the *pri eitz hadar* regarding their need for *hadar*. Thus, there are certain conditions that can invalidate any of the species due to them being considered as having a lack of *hadar*.

Clearly, then, although *hadar* is the defining characteristic of the *pri eitz hadar*, all Arba Minim contain some degree of *hadar*. They are beautiful, and each evinces a certain regality. Although each of the remaining species will be found to possess its own unique quality that evokes a unique form of joy, we should not overlook the common quality of *hadar* and its accompanying form of joy.

SEGMENT 2: PALM FRONDS

We now move to the *kapos temarim*, the frond of a palm tree, also known as the Lulav. Discovering the Lulav's essential joy-stimulating quality requires a bit more thought. In this segment, we will focus on the first and perhaps most obvious uniqueness of the Lulav.

Earlier, we endeavored to establish that the function of waving the species back and forth, as well as up and down, is that of expressing joy and emotion. If this is the case, the need for a specimen with length, significant body-mass, and firmness is a no-brainer. Waving something without any length at all is simply not waving at all. Imagine pumping

---

5   *Sukkah* 31a; *Mishnah Berurah* 645:21.

your hand up and down with a peanut. Are you waving the peanut, or waving your hand while you happen to holding it? While the Aravos and Hadassim admittedly have some length, they are not long or prominent enough to properly express whatever emotion and passion the waver wishes to express.

It is clear that something with some length is needed for this waving exercise. How about a long, thin item? This, too, is lacking in substance. We need something with length *and* body.

How about a long, thick branch? The problem with this is that since it remains straight and cannot be bent at all, waving it does not adequately convey excitement. It's true that something so fragile that it simply falls forward will not do, but neither will something with absolutely no flexibility.

The Lulav, with its bow, is an excellent candidate for this mitzvah. It has the length. It has the body. It has the perfect amount of flexibility and rigidity to make for a meaningful waving exercise.

Note that once the Lulav is present, creating a serious waving experience, the other species are able to become part of that waving experience as well. Though they cannot really be waved on their own, when taken together with the Lulav, they can become part of the greater waving activity.

The Real Rustler

Is the Lulav's uniqueness limited to its length, body, and flexibility? It would seem that there is much more to a Lulav than that.

An introductory question: All of the Arba Minim are waved. When it comes to the Lulav, though, there is an additional act as well. According to many Rishonim,[6] as well as the ruling of the *Rama*[7]—followed by Ashkenazic custom, aside from moving the Lulav back and forth, the Lulav is actually shaken so that its leaves rustle.

---

6   See, for example, *Rambam, Hilchos Lulav* 7:9–10; *Ran to Sukkah* 38a.
7   *Orach Chaim* 651:9.

Though the Rishonim adduce proofs from the Talmud that this is the case, no Biblical source is brought. What is the source of the additional shaking and rustling of the Lulav?

Moreover, what is the meaning and purpose of this movement? Why is it necessary? Why doesn't the back and forth movement, which is how we rejoice with the other three species, suffice for the Lulav as well?

In order to answer these questions, let us consider what we might call the unique "shake-ability" of a Lulav.

Rustling and shaking the Lulav is qualitatively different than shaking any other branch. Shaking a branch causes its leaves to move back and forth, but nothing is being done to the actual branch itself. The Lulav is different. It is actually comprised of a bunch of leaves that together form one unit. When a Lulav is shaken, the body of the Lulav itself opens and closes. The leaves that make up the actual body of the Lulav move about.

Shaking the Lulav causes its very essence to change from one single unit to many leaves and then back again to one unit. The shaking and rustling take place not in appendages of the Lulav, as is the case with other branches or plants, but within the very body of the Lulav itself.

It emerges that the Lulav allows for the optimal rustling experience.

Above, we queried as to the source of the seemingly strange activity of shaking and rustling a Lulav. In the absence of any explanation as to the source of this seemingly strange activity, and in light of what we have discovered as the unique rustling property of the Lulav, we may speculate that the Sages deduced that the reason the Lulav was selected in the first place was for what we will call its unique "shake-ability." After all, a Lulav is a uniquely designed, natural rustling instrument. The Torah's instructing us to "take" a Lulav is in essence an instruction to "take the Lulav and do with it what one is supposed to do with a Lulav," i.e., rustle it!

There is something special—from a purely human perspective, not a religious one—about rustling a Lulav as an expression of joy. Shaking the Lulav, with its attendant satisfaction, is an expression of exuberant joy par excellence.

Fancy Footwork

As we have seen, the Lulav is unique in that it affords us a special shaking/rustling experience. Let us delve into this a bit deeper.

As we saw in chapter 2, movement is an expression of joy, and this accounts for the waving back and forth of the Arba Minim, with which we are enjoined to rejoice.

Rustling, too, is a form of movement. Note the difference, though, between the two types of movement: When an object is waved, the movement does not take place *within* the object but rather happens *to* it. The object is moved from one place to another. Its parts, however, do not move about relative to themselves. When something with parts is shaken, the movement takes place within the object itself. Not only is the Lulav being moved through waving, but when shaken, its very parts move about. When one waves and shakes the Lulav, there is a double movement—a movement within a movement, if you will.

To illustrate this, let us take the example of a person dancing. One part of dancing involves the movement of the dancer from one place to another. Yet a more intense part of the dancing involves the moving about of the dancer's limbs. All of the species *are moved*; yet only the Lulav's "limbs" actually move themselves.

Essentially, this amounts to saying that the active, physical expression of joy exhibited by the Lulav, an expression that is possible only with a Lulav and not with the other species, is greater and more intense than those of the other species.

"And with Shakers…"

While we have endeavored to establish something of the uniqueness of the Lulav, we have for the most part engaged in speculation. Let us look at a Midrash that seems to bear out the correctness of this approach:

In *Shmuel II* (6:5) (the haftarah of *Parashas Shemini*), we read of the event of the bringing of the *Aron* (the Ark of the Covenant) from the land of the Pelishtim to Yerushalayim.[8] There we read:

---

8   Ultimately, that trip was aborted, as a result of the unfortunate death of Uza. The *Aron* was then diverted to Oved Edom's home for a while before being brought to Yerushalayim.

וְדָוִד וְכָל בֵּית יִשְׂרָאֵל מְשַׂחֲקִים לִפְנֵי ה' בְּכֹל עֲצֵי בְרוֹשִׁים וּבְכִנֹּרוֹת וּבִנְבָלִים
וּבְתֻפִּים וּבִמְנַעַנְעִים וּבְצֶלְצֶלִים.

And David and the entire House of Israel were playing before
God with all manner of berosh wood, with violins, with flutes,
and with drums, with menane'im and with cymbals.

Shmuel I 6:5

Translated literally, "*menane'im*" would seem to mean "shakers." What
does this refer to?

The Midrash,[9] commenting on this very verse, explains that "these
refer to Lulavim, which people shake."[10] Indeed, the waving and shaking
of the Lulav is referred to by the Gemara as "*naanu'im*," which has the
same root as *menane'im*.

This Midrash gives us two surprising revelations: First, there is
no indication in this narrative that this event took place on Sukkos.
The Lulavim used here were not religious items being used to fulfill
a mitzvah. Why were they being used?

Clearly, it was considered natural, in times of joy and celebration, to
take up a Lulav and shake it.

The second revelation goes further. The Biblical narrator views the
Lulav as so naturally designed for shaking that it refers to Lulavim as
"shakers." The Lulav's unique "shakability" is definitive of the item.

Shaking a Lulav is not a uniquely religious activity like eating matzoh
or tying tefillin on one's body. The shaking of a Lulav is in and of itself
a deeply human way of expressing joy—exuberant joy. Rather than
inventing a new religious ritual, the Torah has instructed us to utilize
an intuitive, pre-existing expression of joy for the purposes of evoking
the unique spiritual joy that is appropriate for Sukkos.

---

9   *Bamidbar Rabbah* 4:20.

10 It should be noted that numerous Rishonim do not follow the Midrash and instead explain
    that the word "*menane'im*" refers to a particular type of musical instrument, as might be
    indicated by a simple reading of the verse.

Frolicking with the Lulav

Going back to our search for the unique form of joy evoked by each of the Arba Minim, we can now say that the Lulav is designed to evoke an exuberant, celebratory, reveling type of joy. In fact, the verse that used the term "shakers" to refer to Lulavim talked about how the people were "playing" or "frolicking" (*mesachakim*) before God with these and other instruments. It is clear that the joy of the Lulav is one of *sechok*, playing or frolicking.

The act done with the Lulav is perhaps one of expressing joy rather than evoking it. Yet to the point that the Lulav is defined as the instrument of expressing exuberant joy, simply seeing and holding it has the ability to evoke that emotion within the psyche. The Lulav is then waved and rustled in expression of that joy.

Frolicking before God

Once again, we return to our thesis that each form of natural joy is to be utilized in arousing a specific form of sacred joy.

What is the corresponding spiritual joy that is to be aroused in conjunction with the natural form of joy—exuberance—evoked by the Lulav?

Presumably, it is the joy of celebrating and displaying our excitement at our unique relationship with God. If the Esrog is intended to evoke feelings of reverent joy focusing on Hashem's greatness and grandeur, the Lulav ecstatically celebrates our joy at our own relationship with Hashem.

Regression?

What kind of people express joy by shaking things? Children, of course. Better yet, infants. Have you ever seen a mature adult waving something out of excitement? If you have, it's only because that adult is accessing their inner child.

Is this activity of waving a Lulav out of exuberance not beneath our dignity? Since when does the Torah have us engage in childish behaviors?

Perhaps this is exactly the purpose of the mitzvah. It is possible to serve God in many ways, including joy, as in the mitzvah of rejoicing on the Festivals, and yet for none of these to penetrate to the core, to our most primal selves.

Even drinking to intoxication on Purim does not reduce us to children. An inebriated adult is not a child.

With the mitzvah of the Arba Minim, the Torah has us bypass our "adult" selves and express joy in an almost childish way, simply by waving and shaking. We engage the most primal part of ourselves in the celebration and rejoicing.[11]

הילדות הטהורה סופגת היא בקרבה את הטהרה העולמית. חפץ החיים הטהור
בטבעיותו, מפעם הוא בלא זוהמתו רק בלב הילד הטהור. רצון החיים הבלתי מכותם
ומקולקל, הוא זורם בדרך ישרה ממעין החיים, מאוצר החיים העולמי, ומאיר בנשמת
הילדות. הבעת הקודש של הילדות בתומה, כוללת את התמצית היותר חזקה ובהירה
של אידיאליות החיים, ובהתבטאה בקדושה, היא מכשרת את החיים העולמיים
למילוי תפקידם. אין העולם מתקיים אלא בהבל פיהם של תינוקות של בית רבן.

The purity of childhood contains within itself the pure essence of the universe…The sacred expression of childish innocence carries within it the strongest and most powerful essence of the idealism of life, and, when expressed properly, prepares all of life to reach its purpose. [It is for this reason that] "the world exists only in the merits of the Torah studied by young children."[12]

Rav Avraham Yitzchak Kook, Shemoneh Kevatzim 6:284

Impact!

Here, again, let us imagine the impact made on the mind by spending seven days shaking the Lulav, with its full power of expressing

---

11   Of course, there are specific halachos that govern how the Lulav is to be shaken. For that reason, a child is not obligated by the mitzvah of Lulav until he is old enough to shake the Lulav properly (*Sukkah* 42a). Nevertheless, it would appear that at its core, shaking and rustling the Lulav is a child-like activity, though halachah teaches us how to elevate it to a mature form of rejoicing.

12   *Shabbos* 116b.

exuberant joy. The experience would firmly implant in the psyche a powerful sense of celebration at the privilege of serving and relating to God.

Mismatch?

Before continuing our discussion of the Lulav, we might ponder the ostensibly jarring relationship between the Esrog and the Lulav. The Esrog evokes, as we have seen, a more sedate joy born of our awareness of God's greatness as well as our own capacity for attaining Godliness. The Lulav, on the other hand, is the polar opposite of the refined and sedate joy expressed by the Esrog. The joy evoked and expressed by the Lulav is an unabashed, unreserved exuberance. How do these two species go together?

The question is made especially acute in light of our suggestion that the Arba Minim consist of two groups of two, with the Esrog and Lulav functioning together as a pair. How do they work together?

Actually, it would seem that this seeming contradiction is exactly what the Torah has in mind. The two seemingly disparate forms of joy are to offset and complement each other.

Clearly, the Torah sees these two forms of joy not only as not contradictory, but as complementary. The Torah expects us to be able to experience each of these two types of joy to its fullest even as we fully experience the other, seemingly contradictory, type. Moreover, the two types of joy are to be fused together and synthesized to form a deeper, more complex, all-encompassing joy before our Creator.

[The combination of deep solemnity and exuberant rejoicing] is a basic feature of the relationship of God to man...In [some] quarters, [this relationship] is thought of as gloomy and solemn. Therefore [some people] imagine that a way of life such as ours, permeated with the impress of service to God, must be a joyless, stunted existence. They cannot conceive that the spring of the purest joy of life flows from it.

Rav Shamshon Raphael Hirsch, Commentary to Tehillim (47:2)

The One That Is Many

We now return to the Torah's wording in describing the Lulav, "…and a palm frond." Earlier, we propounded the theory that the Torah identifies those characteristics that are the reason for the species' selection. Following along these lines, how does the term *kapos temarim* draw our attention to the Lulav's special "shake-ability?"

The truth is that while we have, once again, followed convention in thus rendering *kapos temarim*, the literal translation of *kapos* is the plural "fronds." Nevertheless, the Talmud observes that the word is written in a way that it could be read as *"kapas,"* the singular "frond." We are therefore left with something of a contradiction between the way the word is written, which would suggest we are to take only one frond, and the way it is actually read, which would suggest taking at least two.

The Talmud (according to one interpretation[13]) addresses this contradiction and resolves it by saying that the Lulav is in fact one object that is made up of many. A Lulav is in actuality not a branch but a leaf of sorts; a leaf that is itself comprised of several leaves. Thus, the word *kapas/kapos* is appropriate for this unusual plant that appears to be one entity, but upon closer examination is discovered to be many.

As we had endeavored to explain, the unique shake-ability of the Lulav is precisely its uniqueness of being one that is many. It is specifically this quality that allows for the optimal rustling experience the Lulav affords. The Torah thus refers to the Lulav as the *kapas/kapos*, the one frond that is in reality many fronds.

Palms of Palms

There is another, startling explanation of the term *kapos temarim*.

Until now, we have followed the conventional renditions of *kapos* as either "branches" or "leaves."

The problem is that there is no Biblical precedent for this usage.

Kapas means "a *kaf* of." What is a *kaf*?

---

13   *Sukkah* 32a, as explained by the *Ritva* there. (*Rashi* offers a different interpretation.) For reasons that are unclear, these comments of the *Ritva* are not found in the *Mossad HaRav Kook* edition. See also Rav S.R. Hirsch, Torah Commentary *Vayikra* (23:40) who cites and elaborates upon the *Ritva's* comments.

Kaf in the Torah is used to mean the palm of the hand, the sole of the foot, or a spoon. Never does the Torah use the word *kaf* to denote a branch.

The *Radak* notes that a related word form, *kipah*, is used in *Neviim* to mean branch. He therefore concludes that *kaf* is a cousin of that form, and indeed means branch.

This seems like a bit of a stretch. Why was this unique word form created specifically for the Lulav? Why is it never used anywhere else?

The *Abarbanel*, apparently disturbed by these questions, offers a terse explanation of his own. Assuming we have correctly understood his intent, it is as follows:

In *Yeshayah*, we read of the trees of the field "clapping their palms (*kaf*)."[14] As the commentaries there explain, this is a metaphor, anthropomorphizing the trees. (In Hebrew, rather than talk about clapping one's "hands," we speak of clapping "palms," which, incidentally, appears more accurate.)

Similarly, in *Tehillim*, we read of the rivers "clapping their palms"[15]— again, of course, a metaphor.

In our context, however, the *Abarbanel* seems to understand that Lulavim themselves are referred to as "palms," or "clappers." The Lulavim, or perhaps more accurately the different parts of the Lulav itself, are the parts of the tree that clap themselves together and make noise.

No other tree is said in *Tanach* to have a *kaf* because, as we have observed, the Lulav is unique in its rustling, clapping nature.

If our understanding of the *Abarbanel's* interpretation is correct, the Torah specifically refers to, and actually describes and singles out, the unique shake-ability of the Lulav. "Take for yourself palm/palms..." Take the hands of the tree and clap them together.[16]

---

14   *Yeshayah* 55:12.

15   *Tehillim* 98:8.

16   It is, of course, difficult to miss the fact that the verse instructs us to "take the palms of palms." The date tree is called a palm, in English as well as a number of other languages, specifically because the Lulavim reaching away from its center give it resemblance to an open palm.

When One Is Not Enough

The Lulav's multiplicity may be significant for another reason as well.

As we discussed in an earlier segment, when someone really wants to express joy, speech and even gesticulation are not enough. It becomes necessary to utilize some object to properly express one's emotion.

What if one object is just not enough?

What if the need to express oneself calls for more? For example, in our context, what if one were to actually sense the teaching of the Midrash, "for every breath one should praise God,"[17] and wish to tangibly express that praise?

One could, of course, take numerous objects, but unless one is an octopus, one is limited in how many objects he can hold and deploy at once.

The Lulav is the perfect solution. In one easily held object, one is actually holding approximately seventy different fronds. Essentially, when you pick up a Lulav, you are picking up seventy palm fronds. (This may be another message conveyed by the tension between the spelling of *kapas temarim*, singular, and the reading of *kapos temarim*, plural. It is one object, but contains within it many, affording the ability to go beyond simply holding one object.)

However, while the Lulav sits inactive, it presents as one item. It is only when it is rustled that it "turns into" many. The act of shaking the Lulav, then, is one of bringing out its full presence as a multiplicity of fronds. When we want to actively praise Hashem with it, we shake it, turning it into many, many fronds, and use each and every one of them, individually, to express that praise.

Part 2: Hadassim and Aravos

SEGMENT 1: THE FROND OF A PLAITED TREE

Symmetry of Fullness

The third species is that of *anaf eitz avos*, a frond of a plaited tree, known to us as a Hadas, or myrtle branch. In keeping with our understanding that the Torah identifies the salient characteristics of each species, let us examine the specifications of this plant. At the simplest

---

17   *Bereishis Rabbah* 14:9.

level, the word "*avos*" means "thickness." In our context it refers to the abundance of leaves, which creates an impression of fullness. The Gemara (*Sukkah* 32b) derives another two criteria from the words *anaf eitz avos*:

- From the word "*avos*" we derive that it must be plaited, which the Gemara interprets to mean that the three leaves of each pod must be exactly parallel to each other.
- From the juxtaposition of the words "frond" and "tree," we derive that the entire branch must be covered by leaves, as contrasted with most branches that have only sporadic, uneven growth of leaves.

In more abstract terms, the *anaf eitz avos* must have (1) an abundance of leaves, (2) symmetry, and (3) fullness.

The fact that symmetry is a salient factor brought to the equation of the species by the Hadas is borne out by another phenomenon as well.

Halachah follows the opinion that three Hadas branches are to be taken.[18] Some of the earlier as well as later commentators suggest that the Sages understood the word "plaited" as referring not only to the actual branch's being plaited by a trilogy of leaves, but to the branches themselves as forming a trilogy of branches.[19]

Essentially, according to this interpretation, there is no intrinsic need for three Hadas branches; one should suffice, just as only one Esrog and only one Lulav are needed. Rather, the Hadas' unique quality of plaited-ness must find expression not only in the form of its leaves, but in the formation of a Hadas bouquet.

Gazing at and contemplating a Hadas, one notices the feeling of multiplicity, the symmetry, and the fullness it engenders.

The Hadas's unique arrangement gives it a unique beauty, one that borders on the beauty of a flower.

The Esrog and Lulav can certainly be described as beautiful. Their beauty, however, is not their primary characteristic. It plays a secondary

---

18   *Orach Chaim* 651:1.
19   *Piskei HaRid*, *Sukkah* 34b; *Rashash* ad loc.; see also *Rashi*, *Sukkah* 45a s.v. *ba'avosim* (all of these sources referenced by the *sefer Ben Melech*).

role, with their distinguishing features being those of grandeur and an expression of exuberant joy, respectively. Neither represent beauty for the sake of beauty.

The joy of the Hadas, it would appear, is closer to the joy brought about by pure beauty; specifically, the ingredients of beauty that are richness, intricacy, and perfection.

Once again, it is important to reiterate that we are not referring to what the Hadas represents or symbolizes. Seeing something symmetric engenders a feeling of symmetry within, and the same is true of other qualities. When we look at and interact with the myrtle branches, with their symmetry and beauty, our sensitivities to these values are awakened and stimulated.

Divine Intricacy

What aspect of the Jew's relationship with his Creator is expressed in the joy of perfection, symmetry, and beauty?

God is the One source from which emanates infinite fullness and richness. "How great are Your works, O God," is explained by Rabbi Akiva to mean,[20] how diverse are your works, and by Rav Saadiah Gaon as, how complex are your works.[21] Hashem is introduced to us in *Bereishis* as Elokim, but is later, only once creation has been completed, referred to as Hashem Elokim. In the words of the Sages, "Hashem's full name is mentioned only in conjunction with the fullness of creation."[22]

Complexity, intricacy, perfection, and beauty are evident both in the creation of Hashem, as well as in His Torah and mitzvos. In the Torah we perceive perfection; the symmetry of its many laws and their effect on us; its all-pervasive nature that leaves nothing untouched; and the beauty of Torah life.

The fullness, beauty, and intricacy of the Hadassim, experienced within the context of our relationship with Hashem, allow us to tap into fullness, beauty, and intricacy of Hashem Himself, as it were,

---

20   *Chullin* 127a.
21   *Ha'Emunos V'HaDei'os* 4:2.
22   *Bereishis Rabbah* 13:3.

as expressed through His handiwork and His Torah. By taking the Hadas, yet another dimension of joy is introduced into our relationship with God.

SEGMENT 2: WILLOWS OF THE BROOK

The fourth and last of the species is perhaps the most difficult to appreciate. The Aravah is a simple, relatively non-descript willow branch. What about it engenders joy, and what unique quality does it bring with it?

Here, once again, we take our cue from the wording of the Torah. The Aravos are referred to as *arvei nachal*, willows of a brook. Halachically, Aravos need not grow on the banks of a brook to be kosher; provided they are of the right species, it does not matter where they have grown (*Sukkah* 33b-34a).[23] Nevertheless, the Torah refers to them as brook-willows; as Rishonim explain, only those types of willows that usually do grow by brooks are acceptable.[24] Why the emphasis on water and brooks?

Clearly, although it does not matter where the Aravos grow, it is their association with water—with the brook—that makes them desirable. The species generally grows by water, and in the mind's eye, Aravos and water go hand in hand.

Anyone who has seen willows growing by a brook understands that the relationship between the willows and the brook is profound. Often, the branches will grow in a manner such that the willows actually hang over, or sometimes even into, the waters of the brook.

To someone used to seeing brook-willows in their natural habitat, willows and brooks are simply inseparable. For such a person, merely seeing or holding the Aravos immediately evokes the image of them growing over the brook. Wherever Aravos are, they are "willows of the brook."

---

23   According to some opinions, it is indeed optimal to use Aravos that actually grew by a brook. See *Mishnah Berurah* 647:3.

24   *Rambam Hilchos Lulav*, 7:3; *Ritva, Sukkah* 33b.

Life at Its Source

What is the unique joy of *arvei nachal*?

Water is the source of all life. Every living thing needs water to grow. However, this is most evident in *arvei nachal* where we can actually see and experience the direct connection between the plant and the water. Seeing the Aravos growing directly next to the brook—and we have argued that the Aravah brings this image with it wherever it goes—gives us a snapshot of life emanating from its source.

The joy aroused by *arvei nachal* is the simplest and most basic form of joy—the joy of life itself.

It is not only water per se with which the Torah seeks association. The emphasis is on the *nachal*, the brook, which, as the Talmud notes (*Sukkah* 33b), flows. The Torah is not interested in the pacifying effect of the placid lake or pond that have nowhere to go and nothing to do; nor does it want the busy bustle of the raging river. It is toward the calm but vibrant flow of the bubbling brook that the Torah focuses our attention.

While Aravos awaken association with brooks, it is important to note that the Aravos do not serve simply as a vehicle to remind us of brooks. Rather, the Aravah itself, against the background of the brook, takes on a new character. It is as if the life-giving properties of growth, tranquility, and plentitude of the brook, have been transposed into the Aravah. The Aravah, with its added life and simple beauty, now itself contains, so to speak, the entire gamut of joy-evoking properties of the brook.

Aravos, simply by dint of the way they grow, are viewed as plant life that is a direct extension of water, and hence evoke the various components of joy we associate with the brook.

It is interesting to note that the Aravah, the one species associated by the Torah with something outside of itself, is also the simplest of all the species. On its own, it is relatively unremarkable; perhaps its very simplicity and unassuming nature are what make it the perfect vehicle for expressing the vitality of the brook.

Furthermore, as the species designed to express the simple joy of vitality, the Aravah, with its no-frills character, expresses the most basic of all joys: the joy of simply being alive.

In our general discussion of the ability of aesthetically pleasing plants to elicit joy, we viewed *Rashi's* comment to *Mishlei* (15:30). The verse there states, "The light of the eyes gladdens the heart." *Rashi* explains, "The light of the eyes, i.e., something that is attractive to the eyes, such as gardens of greenery and flowing rivers, gladdens the heart."

Arvei nachal, of course, incorporates both the greenery as well as the flowing river. It is truly "the light of the eyes."

The Living God

What type of spiritual joy is to be aroused by the natural joy evoked by the Aravos?

God, Who is, of course, the Ultimate Source of all life, is even referred to as "the God of Life." And as the Torah reminds us repeatedly, it is only God's mitzvos that assure us true life. As the Torah states, "These are the commandments that man shall do in order to *live* through them."[25] And it is a connection to and relationship with Hashem that allows for real growth and authentic tranquility. It is thus reasonable to suggest that it is precisely the joy felt in the presence of the source of all of these basic and necessary qualities.

Balance

Let us now return to our earlier assertion that the Arba Minim are to be divided into two duos: Esrog-Lulav, Hadassim-Aravos. Let us explore the relationship between the Hadassim and Aravos.

If the Hadassim elicit a joy of richness, of complexity and intricacy, the Aravos serve as a foil for that form of joy. The Aravos have little to offer aside from their own simple aliveness and their association with the brook by which they grow. It's their plainness that evokes the joy of simplicity—the simple joy of being alive.

Is joy to be found in the simplicity of life, or is it in the intricacy and complexity we find in the world? A corollary of this question in the spiritual realm: Is spiritual joy to be found in the simplicity of the physical and spiritual life bequeathed upon us by our Creator, or is it found in appreciating the complexities of Torah and the intricacies of

---

25   *Vayikra* 18:5.

the mitzvos? Of course, both extremes are necessary; each offsets the other. This is the ostensible tension between the Hadassim and Aravos, a tension that is resolved only by striking the proper balance between the two approaches.

הלחץ הפנימי לעלייה תמידית בתורה ועבודה ממעט את גודל השמחה האצורה בעובדה הפשוטה של "היות יהודי," בלי מדריגות מיוחדות של עליה. ובכל זה, הרי שמחת עולמים הכלולה בעובדה פשוטה זו צריכה להיות שופעת בצינורי הנפש. ומבחינה ידועה הרי היא תנאי מוקדם לעבודת השגת המדרגות...והרי זו חובה מיוחדת על העובד, שהרדיפה אחר השגת המדריגות לא תחליש בקרבו את השמחה הכלולה במצב של היות יהודי בלי מדריגיות.

The inner drive to constantly grow in Torah and Divine service can weaken the great joy inherent in the very fact that one is a Jew...Nevertheless, this eternal joy must always be flowing through the pipelines of the soul...There is a special responsibility incumbent upon one who aspires to high levels of spirituality, to see to it that his pursuit of high levels does not weaken within himself the joy inherent in simply being a Jew.

Rav Yitzchak Hutner, Sefer HaZikaron p. 71

Part 3: When Trees Are Waved

There is another aspect of the joy of the Arba Minim that deserves to be investigated.[26]

Examination of the relevant verse reveals that the Torah puts a great deal of focus on the host tree of each species. For example, the Torah speaks not of a fruit of *hadar*, but of "the fruit of a *hadar* tree." It speaks not of a plaited frond, but of the frond of a plaited tree. Why the emphasis on the tree?

It would seem that at a certain level, the essence of the mitzvah is actually to use the various *trees*, not the parts that we actually shake, to rejoice before God. Thus, for example, we are not shaking an Esrog

---

26   This chapter is based on the *sefer Ben Melech: Sukkos*, pp. 68–79.

per se, but rather a representative of the Esrog tree, and in doing so we conceptually use the Esrog tree itself to rejoice before and praise God.

The trees were selected based on their own importance:

- The Esrog tree is unique in its beauty because of the beautiful fruit it carries. (It is also unique in other ways, as the Talmud (*Sukkah* 35a) points out: It bears fruit throughout the year unlike other fruit trees, and it bears all sorts of sizes of fruits.)
- The palm tree stands regal as the tallest of the fruit tree. (It is also bare until the very top, which serves to accentuate its height.) According to one reading of the *Talmud Yerushalmi*, this very reason is given for the selection of the Lulav. The very word for a palm tree—*tamar*—means standing tall, and is used precisely because the palm tree stands tall.
- The myrtle tree is beautiful in that it is completely covered with plaited branches.
- The willow tree is unique in that it grows adjacent to water.

Adapting this to our general approach, we might say that the joy is one borne of the aesthetic experience of the trees themselves. Through taking up and handling the species, our focus is turned to their sources, the trees themselves, and this focus allows for a more intensive involvement with the joy-inducing properties of each species.

Even within the facet of focusing on the trees themselves, the specific part of each tree was selected not arbitrarily, but as a way of expressing the uniqueness of its host tree:

- The Esrog is what makes the Esrog tree beautiful. We wish to wave the tree because it is beautiful; we wave the very part that makes the tree beautiful.
- The Lulav grows from the highest part of the palm tree. This, together with the Lulav's own height, makes it the best candidate to express the tree's height.
- The uniqueness of the Hadas tree, its covering with plaited branches, is of course best expressed through those branches themselves.

- The Talmud states that the leaves of the Aravah are elongated so that they themselves are shaped like a brook.[27] The Aravah trees proximity to the brook, which characterizes its uniqueness, is thus expressed by the Aravah branch itself.

We may view the focus on the host trees in a slightly more cerebral fashion as well. Immersing ourselves in the appearance of each of the species has a profound impact on our senses. However, the added focus on the host trees, and their abstract uniqueness, adds a slightly more mature element. It is as if we tap into the concept behind them and utilize it to praise and rejoice before God.

SINGING TREES (3)

As we have seen earlier on, the Midrash applies the verse that speaks of "singing trees" to the mitzvah of the Arba Minim. Note that the verse does not speak of singing tree branches but rather singing trees. The implication is that not only do the species that we take into our hands serve to praise God, but even the trees from which they come.

Based on what we have seen in this chapter, the verse's emphasis on the trees themselves becomes eminently understandable. The higher level of fulfillment of this mitzvah is by relating not only to the species used to fulfill it, but to their host trees as well. By shaking the species with an awareness of the trees they represent, we cause the trees themselves to sing out, as it were.

By instructing us to utilize natural species to praise God, the Torah teaches us that the joy and praise expressed by taking up these species is an all-encompassing one. We are to experience it as if nature itself is praising and rejoicing before God.

Nature does, after all, by its very existence, bear testimony to God's greatness, as the verse states, "The heavens relate the glory of God, and the firmament bespeaks of His handiwork."[28] Of course, it is primarily through the agency of human consciousness that this praise takes place.

---

27   *Sukkah* 33b.
28   *Tehillim* 19:2.

With the mitzvah of the Arba Minim, human beings actively experience the song inherent in nature's very existence.

MORE ON PALMS[29]

The only one of the four trees that the Torah has us focus on for its own sake is the palm tree. The Esrog tree is unique because of its Esrogim; the Hadas tree because it's covered with Hadassim; the Aravah because of where it grows. It is only the palm tree that is named explicitly and is apparently important in its own right.

What is so special about the palm tree?

Contemplating a palm tree, the first thing we notice is that it has personality! Most other trees can blend in with each other, creating an undifferentiated canopy of leaves and branches. Not so a palm; it stands alone.

Palm trees generally stand straight, as opposed to other trees that twist and turn and don't always seem to know where they're headed. Actually, this fact is noted by the Sages. On the verse in *Shir Hashirim* (7:8), "She (i.e., the Jewish People) is like a palm," *Rashi* explains, "We saw the beauty of [Yisrael's] stature in the days of Nevuchadnetzar, when all the nations were kneeling and falling before the image, but you stood as erect as this palm tree."

Columns of smoke are called by the Navi (*Yoel* 3:3) "*timros ashan;*" in the words of the *Radak*, "Since a palm is a tall, straight, and even tree, the Navi compares anything tall and straight to it."

In the idiom of the Sages, saying that something is "*metamer ve'oleh*" means that it stands in a straight and tall column.[30]

The palm tree, then, has become the very symbol for something tall and straight.

Going further, a palm tree has a head, while other trees simply have branches growing randomly, with nothing unique about their tops.

In fact, it is specifically the palm's head that accentuates its height. While many trees grow tall, the palm tree's bareness until its top

---

29   Based on *sefer Ben Melech* referenced above.
30   See, for example, *Yoma* 38a.

draws the observer's attention to its head, so that its height makes an immediate impression.

Is it any wonder that the Torah chose the palm tree as the leader of the Arba Minim? We are to come with the full power of persuasion of the palm tree and wave its representative in exuberant joy before Hashem.[31]

BRANCHING OUT

Joy, the *Maharal* explains,[32] is another way of saying "open." When a person is sad, he retreats from others. When he is happy, he opens up and lets others in. This phenomenon finds expression in the way the Sages refer to the two types of *tefachim*, handbreadths.[33] The smaller handbreath is referred to as a "sad *tefach*," while the larger one is called "the smiling *tefach*." *Simchah* (joy) opens us and expands ourselves.

One of the unique properties of the palm tree is the way its fronds fall away from the center. In a sense, the palm tree unfurls itself to the greatest extent possible. It projects an image of expansiveness and receptivity.

Here, again, the Lulav, a representative of the palm tree, carries within it expression of its host tree. The Lulav itself appears to be a closed frond, but, when waved and rustled, opens and expands itself. Unlike the palm tree, which opens by itself, the Lulav must be "operated" in order to open up. The "operator" actually has a part in expanding the Lulav. He is essentially utilizing the Lulav to express his own expansive state of joy. This would appear to be yet another way in which the Lulav functions as an instrument of rejoicing par excellence.

---

31 The palm tree projects an image of values so necessary in proper Divine service: its height directs our attention Heavenward, and its straightness reminds us of the righteous, who are called (*Tehillim* 97:11) "those straight in their hearts." And our request of Hashem is that He bring us back "standing straight to our land." Does the Torah's selection of this tree have anything to do with this? We can only speculate.

32 *Nesivos Olam, Nesiv Gemilus Chassadim* 4.

33 See *Eiruvin* 3b.

Integration

In summary, we have discovered four types of natural joy associated with the Arba Minim, each of which, we have suggested, is designed to arouse a corresponding form of spiritual joy:

- **Esrog:** The joy of splendor, of refined beauty; a possible reflection of our joy at attaining greatness and at finding ourselves in the presence of the ultimate grandeur of God.
- **Lulav:** Exuberant, celebratory joy; a possible reflection of our own ecstatic joy at being members of Hashem's People.
- **Hadas:** The joy of fullness, of complexity and beauty; a possible reflection of our joyous appreciation of the fullness, complexity, and beauty expressed in the natural world as well as the Torah.
- **Aravah:** The joy of life, growth, and vitality; possibly expressive of the joy of life, growth, and tranquility that come along with being in Hashem's presence and keeping the Torah.

The mitzvah of the Arba Minim, if we have understood it correctly, recognizes and encourages the central importance of all four types of joy in our relationship with God and Torah.

Yet we would be remiss to think that the mitzvah takes four unrelated types of joys and lumps them together. The very form of the mitzvah would suggest that the mitzvah sees all four of these forms of joy as various aspects of one all-encompassing form of spiritual joy, one that should govern and pervade our relationship with Hashem and Torah.

Moreover, each individual form of spiritual joy is enhanced and transformed by being incorporated into a whole containing all four of these joys. There is a cross-pollination between the various types of joy; each borrows aspects from the other forms of joy, giving each form added contour and depth.

Why Not Flowers — Second Round

Having attempted to work out a theory explaining the unique desirability of the Arba Minim in evoking and expressing spiritual joy, we need to return to a question we raised earlier, namely, why not flowers?

We need to tread carefully here, and to ask the flower-loving part of ourselves not to take offense, as indeed no offense is meant. The same God Who apparently eschewed flowers for the purposes of this mitzvah, is the God Who created flowers in all their spectacular variety and beauty. Clearly, flowers play a significant role in life, but not for this particular mitzvah. Why not?

Think about flowers and the joy they precipitate. What kind of joy is it?

The most outstanding characteristic of flowers is, of course, beauty.

Beauty can be intoxicating. It can convince us of its own intrinsic value, causing us to lose focus on the values it is supposed to awaken us to. Instead of using beauty to get us to a more transcendent state, we may tend to get stuck with the beauty itself.

Flowers indicate for us beauty for the sake of beauty—or otherwise put—all show and no content. When we say that an essay or speech is "flowery," we mean, in the words of the dictionary, that it is "full of ornate and grandiloquent expressions; highly embellished." With no offense meant to flowers, it seems that they have become the very symbol of unnecessary pretense; of artifice; of form without content.

At a pragmatic level, flowers are important to have around. They anesthetize us to our pain; they can even energize us. Perhaps, though, they do not elevate us to higher, more pristine levels of existence. Important as flowers are, they should be utilized for their more natural potential. Activating spiritual joy requires something else altogether.

The Beauty of Holiness

Even when the Torah focuses our attention on natural beauty for the sake of facilitating spiritual joy, it is careful to avoid anything that could lead us to ascribe inherent value or sanctity to beauty.

Indeed, as we saw earlier, halachah demands that all the species meet the criterion of "*Hadar*." *Hadar*, we argued in a previous segment, refers to something closer to majesty than to beauty—or at least a type of beauty that borders on majesty or nobility. Rather than beauty for its own sake, the beauty utilized by the Torah is one of *Hadar*, of grandeur and reverence, communicating an understated beauty whose attraction lies more in its intimation of what it represents, than in what it actually meets the eye. The beauty of *Hadar* more readily facilitates the bridge between man's aesthetic faculties and his spiritual receptivity, and it more closely approaches the meeting point between the physical and the spiritual. In sensitizing man to the notion that beauty approaches nobility of spirit, it prepares man to grasp the notion that nobility—sanctity—is itself beautiful.

> The Greeks believed in the holiness of beauty…Jews believed in the opposite: *hadrat kodesh*, the beauty of holiness.
>
> *Rabbi Jonathan Sacks, Covenant and Conversation, Vayakhel 5779*
>
> For the Greeks, what was beautiful was holy; for the Jews, what was holy was beautiful.
>
> *Rabbi Ken Spiro, Crash-Course in Jewish History p. 147*

More on the Beauty of Holiness

These reflections on "the beauty of holiness" lead us to ponder another question.

What impact is the mitzvah of the Arba Minim meant to leave upon us as people, as human beings?

We have already examined various possible ways in which the mitzvah is to impact us in terms of our associations with nature, God, and Torah. But perhaps the mitzvah's impact is not limited to associations? Is it possible that it seeks to change us to our very core?

As human beings, we are constantly engaged in a struggle between two warring forces. Left unattended, we tend to gravitate toward immediate physical gratification, egotistical and egocentric strivings, and short-sightedness. Yet if we dig deeper, we hear the call of nobility. Deep down we sense that there is something higher, something more elevated to life. We can choose to follow the call of our higher selves, to transcend pettiness and ascend to a life of elevation and greatness.

For seven days, the Torah has made the species, with their combination of vitality, beauty, and nobility, the focal point of our rejoicing before God. Moreover, it has ordained that for these seven days we focus on God's beauty and nobility, as it were. In doing so, we send our psyches a continuous stream of messages that life is about achieving nobility and the deeper joy that comes with it. Ideally, we emerge from the fulfillment of this mitzvah ennobled and as more elevated human beings.

אהבת היופי היא מדה יפה...אבל צריך להשתמש במדה זו כמו בכל המידות הטובות: לשם שמים! כגון, להכיר ביופי הבריאה את הבורא, להיות נפש בין אדם לחבירו...

An appreciation for beauty is a positive trait. However, it must be utilized, like all positive traits, for the sake of Heaven. For example, recognizing the Creator through the beauty of Creation, or developing the "beauty of the soul," which is necessary to excel in interpersonal relationships.

Rabbi Shlomo Wolbe, Collected Letters, vol. 2, no. 276

CHAPTER 5

Consolidating

Having formulated a basic understanding of the process by which the Torah wishes the Arba Minim to bring us to specific forms of spiritual joy, let us look at some of the ways in which this would impact us.

As we noted above in the context of the Esrog, one phenomenon that might occur when we combine natural and spiritual joy is that our higher spiritual joy is drawn into the lower, more primal parts of our personality.

The human being is made up of various different parts. We have a Godly soul, an intellect, emotions, instincts, physical desires, and corporeal bodies. We may have developed a love and appreciation for serving God, but that appreciation may be confined to our souls or minds; it may not have penetrated to our lower levels of existence.

Until we performed the mitzvah of the Arba Minim, perhaps our spiritual, cerebral sides knew how to be happy about our relationship with God and His Torah, but not our natural, human sides. But for man to be truly connected to God, all aspects of his personality must be engaged; this is facilitated by the mitzvah of the Arba Minim. The mitzvah allows the lower, simpler parts of our existence to experience that joy.

Focal Point
As we have seen, the Arba Minim in general, and each species in particular, leave a powerful impression on the human psyche.

It is important to note that the impact of the Arba Minim is not limited to the simple act of lifting and waving them. The species become the focus of our activity for seven days. We recite *Hallel* with them daily, using them to express the emotions of joy and thanksgiving aroused by *Hallel*.

At the Pesach Seder, we have divinely ordained centerpieces. These are "props" to create the appropriate atmosphere in which to relate and relive the Exodus from Egypt.[1] Correspondingly, on Sukkos, our divinely ordained centerpiece is that of the Arba Minim.

Even aside from the actual time spent with them, the species occupy a central role in our consciousness for these seven days (and even before the seven days, when we are preparing for the mitzvah). They, with all their associations and an awareness of their context, become the focus of our attention. The mitzvah of taking and waving the species, expressive as it is of a general mood that should pervade our consciousness, comes to express and define the very essence of this time period. The species become the lens through which we peer at life for these four days. The days of Sukkos themselves become, in our consciousness, days defined by the emotions and moods expressed by the Arba Minim, exponentially multiplying the impression the species leave on our psyches.

Rav Yechezkel Abramsky used to leave his Minim in a vase of fresh water, displayed in a place of prominence throughout the day on Sukkos.[2]

Rav Chaim Brim, B'Ohr Panecha: Sukkos

---

1. See *Michtav Me'Eliyahu*, vol. 4, p. 255.
2. Obviously, there is no technical fulfillment of the mitzvah to be had by simply gazing at the Arba Minim; yet it may be suggested that doing so is within the spirit of the mitzvah. See *Mesilas Yesharim* chap. 19 for a discussion on the virtues of extrapolating from the mitzvos based on their underlying themes.

The People of Yerushalayim

Earlier, we looked at the practice of the *Anshei Yerushalayim* who would hold on to the species throughout the day.

As we mentioned there, Rishonim make it clear that holding onto the Minim constituted an added fulfillment of the mitzvah of the species.

In a way, the mitzvah of the Arba Minim lends itself to this behavior more than any other mitzvah. Once one has blown a shofar, for example, it is not really possible to continue the fulfillment of the mitzvah. The same is true of eating matzoh. But with taking the Arba Minim, it is possible to stretch out the fulfillment of the mitzvah to the point that it accompanies a person throughout his day.

Why is this so? Why are some mitzvos over once the act has been performed, while the fulfillment of the mitzvah of the Arba Minim may be continued?

To answer this, let us contemplate the following question: What were the *Anshei Yerushalayim* doing with the species? Were they going about their activities as usual while taking advantage of the easy opportunity to gain another mitzvah by just holding the species in their hands?

Perhaps. But we may also suggest that by holding the species throughout whatever it was they were doing, all their activities became colored by the encounter with the species. The respective attitudes and moods conveyed by each of the species were, in this way, injected into all of their encounters with other people, Hashem, and any situations that came their way. For a day, or possibly seven days, they practiced seeing all of life through the lenses of the Esrog, Lulav, Hadassim, and Aravos.

It would seem, then, that the conduct of *Anshei Yerushalayim* exemplifies what it is that the Torah wants us to be doing with the species. "Take them," the Torah says; meaning, make them a constant companion during these seven days.

Take to Yourselves

Up until this point we have regarded the mitzvah of the Arba Minim as primarily one of creating a certain effect on the human psyche. However, there is an additional, possibly deeper, aspect of this mitzvah.

Let us contemplate the uniqueness of this mitzvah, which one can technically discharge simply by taking the species into his hands. What is the meaning of the act of "taking"? What is one actually doing when one takes something into his hands?

Aside from the species' serving as stimuli of joy aroused at their sight and presence, the mandate to take them up establishes a certain degree of fusion between them and the person taking them. To a certain extent it seems almost as if the mitzvah is telling us to install the species within our personae. It is telling us to become one with each of the species. It instructs us to allow our personae to become defined by the species. The mitzvah of Lulav instructs us to reinvent ourselves as people whose very essence is defined by the beauty, regality, vitality, symmetry, and exuberance contained in the species.

"*U'lekachtem lachem*," normally translated as "take for yourselves," can also be translated as "take to or toward yourselves." The Torah is asking us to become people who contain within themselves a "fruit of a *hadar* tree," a "palm branch," a "frond of a plaited tree," and a "brook-willow."

Externalization

In an earlier chapter we talked about how taking the species acts both as a catalyst to joy, as well as a way of expressing joy. That is, the mitzvah of taking the species has both inward-bound as well as outward-bound aspects.

In the previous chapter we suggested that the inward-bound act, beyond merely arousing joy, involves incorporating the values represented by the species into one's personality. What is the parallel outward-bound act?

We can suggest that, inasmuch as the four types of joy are four types of inner experiences, the Arba Minim act as a concrete expression of those four inner types of experiences. If a person is currently experiencing these attitudes and emotions, he will automatically view taking up these species as one of crystallizing those feelings in a physical manner. The species themselves become, in his eyes, physical manifestations of his inner experience.

(Perhaps this is another reason for the requirement that one own the species used to fulfill the mitzvah. For it to be seen as a crystallization of one's inner reality, it must be an extension of oneself, i.e., one's property.)

The Art of Subtlety

Even with all of the explanation we have offered, some lingering doubt may remain: Is simply handling the Arba Minim the best way to make a significant impact on the psyche?

If the purpose of the mitzvah is to utilize nature's joy-inducing properties to evoke positive spiritual associations, surely the impact would be more profound if we were to surround ourselves with an abundance of these species. Wouldn't spending seven days in an orchard make an even stronger impression? Or perhaps we could split our time: two days in an Esrog orchard, two where Lulavim grow, two with Hadassim, and one day wandering the brooks gazing at the Aravos?

There are a number of possible answers to this, all having to do with the Torah's understanding of human nature and its program of influencing it.

First, the Torah may be telling us that being surrounded is not the same as being actively involved. It is the actual involvement and activity with the Minim, and most specifically activating them in the presence of Hashem, that sears their properties into our minds.

But there is another secret contained here.

The strongest experience is one that demands cerebral involvement. Emotional experiences may feel strong at the time they occur, but they are "easy come, easy go." Little remains of them. A more authentic experience is one that requires the participation of the mind. Having to work toward an emotional experience makes the experience not only more real, but more permanent.

Rav Yosef Yehudah Bloch, in his *Shiurei Daas*,[3] addresses this issue at a general level. He points out that the conscious mind, along with the senses, can serve as a filter, soaking up all the effects of that which we see

---

3   Vol. I, "*Nishmas HaTorah.*"

and do. This can result in our being deeply affected at a superficial level, but not being affected at all at a deeper level or on a long-term basis.

In order for things to filter through to our subconscious mind, Rav Bloch explains, it is necessary to engage consistently in small, quiet acts that do not make a huge impression on the senses or the conscious mind. Paradoxically, it is specifically these acts and messages which embed themselves into the deeper parts of our psyches and remain there.

Rav Bloch points out that doing loud and highly impressive acts might have a strong immediate effect, but they don't have much lasting influence. Their flashiness stirs a person's lower faculties but because the impression is so extensive on the superficial level it never reaches and really penetrates the higher subtler faculties.

The species may be beautiful and joy-evoking, each in its own way. Yet it certainly cannot be denied that their aesthetic power is subtle; one must use his mind to bring out their full power. Focus is called for to properly appreciate their beauty and to allow it to evoke the corresponding emotions within the psyche. An aesthetic experience that calls for active involvement leaves a deeper impression than just seeing even the most overpowering sight.

It is specifically the unique partnership between mind and emotion that allows the emotions generated by the handling of and involvement with the species to fully penetrate every corner of our consciousness.

CHAPTER 6

Before God

There are many categories of mitzvos, each with its own unique nature. It is important to recognize the different categories of mitzvos in order to grasp the unique nature and function of each mitzvah.

While all mitzvos connect us to God, there are different ways of doing so, and therefore different types of mitzvos. One well known division of mitzvos is that of categorizing all mitzvos as either *bein adam la'Makom*, between man and God; *bein adam l'chaveiro*, between man and his fellow; and *bein adam l'atzmo*, between man and himself, that is, those mitzvos that mold a person's character.

It would seem that the category of *bein adam la'Makom* could be further broken down into two subcategories. Some involve a direct engagement with God, while others, though directly related to our relationship with God, do not.

As an example, reciting the *Shema* and praying are both mitzvos that have to do with our relationship with God. There is, however, an essential difference between them. While reciting the *Shema* strengthens our awareness of our responsibilities to God, one is not actually communicating with God while reading the *Shema*.[1] Prayer, on the other hand,

---

1   In fact, the *Tur* (*Orach Chaim* 61) compares reading the *Shema* to reading a letter addressed to a person by a king. This is a different experience than standing before the king and interacting with him directly.

does; for what is the essence of prayer if not standing before God and speaking to Him?

For this reason, while one must be fully dressed before praying, the halachah is more relaxed when it comes to reciting the *Shema*.[2] As *Rashi* explains, when one prays, he "stands before the King," but the same is not true of reciting the *Shema*.[3] It is God's will, and it is all about God. But essentially, reciting *Shema* is about a person accepting certain tenets upon himself and does not require God's presence or interaction.

Another example is the commandment to confess when one has transgressed. As the *Rambam* writes, confessing one's sins must be done "before Hashem."[4] If one verbally enumerates his sins, but not as a way of communicating with, or in the presence of, God, he has not fulfilled this mitzvah.

What about our mitzvah? Where does it fit in?

Note that the way the mitzvah is expressed by the Torah is, "take the species and rejoice before God." While the Sages explain[5] that this refers to the mitzvah to take the species in the Mikdash, a geographical location that is before God, the plain meaning of the verse is that the very essence of this mitzvah is one that needs to be performed in God's presence. Although Hashem is, of course, present everywhere, the Torah would seem to be calling, for the purposes of this particular mitzvah, for a heightened awareness of the fact that one is standing before Hashem.[6]

The Silent Partner

Having postulated that the mitzvah of the Arba Minim is one that is to be performed "before Hashem," let us examine what practical implications this has for how we fulfill the mitzvah.

---

2   See *Berachos* 24b–25a.
3   *Berachos* 25a, s.v. *aval*.
4   *Hilchos Teshuvah*, 1:1.
5   *Toras Kohanim*, cited by *Rashi*, *Sukkah* 41, s.v. *baMikdash*.
6   This is further indicated by the wording "before Hashem, your God." Generally, when the Torah wishes to convey the fact that a given mitzvah applies only in the Beis Hamikdash, or only in Yerushalayim, it states only "before Hashem." The wording of "before Hashem, your God," suggests an element of the relationship between the person and God, indicating that the Torah wishes the person to feel that he is actually before God, wherever he happens to be.

In order to do this, we need to first investigate why this mitzvah should be different than most others. We understand that the mitzvah of prayer, for example, requires God's presence. Its very definition is communicating with Hashem; it cannot be done solo. The same is true of confession and repentance. But why should the Lulav fit into this category?

The answer may have to do with the nature and essence of the mitzvah. As we have already established, the essence of the mitzvah of the Arba Minim is to rejoice using very specific "props." Note that there is also another mitzvah in the Torah involving rejoicing: the mitzvah to be happy on the *Regalim*. This mitzvah does not require the "presence" of God; it is enough to rejoice on one's own, focusing on our relationship with God and the blessings He has bestowed upon us. The rejoicing of the Lulav, though, is of a different flavor. It is not a general state of mind, but an active and dynamic expression of acute joy.

Assuming our postulation about Lulav requiring the presence of God is correct, we may suggest that the very meaning and significance of this activity is that of actively rejoicing in the presence of God. It is as if the Creator Himself, as it were, is a passive participant in this mitzvah. Much as one cannot pray without God filling His role as Listener, one cannot rustle the Lulav without the One before, and to Whom, the Lulav is being rustled.

Think of wedding guests dancing before a bride and groom. Were the bride and groom to exit the room, the dancing would become devoid of meaning. The celebratory movement of waving the species has meaning only when done in the presence of, and perhaps even interacting with, God.

Ultimate Destination

As we have observed numerous times, the mitzvah of the Arba Minim serves as the culmination and climax of our spiritual year. It seems entirely apropos that this mitzvah is performed "before God." Our ultimate destination, the place we are all striving toward, is precisely the position of standing before Hashem. "I shall walk before Hashem in the land of life" (*Tehillim* 116:9). The only possible response to arriving at that destination is "rejoicing before God."

A New Perspective

The notion of performing the mitzvah of the Arba Minim "before Hashem" animates the mitzvah in a completely new way. Every aspect of it would take on immeasurably deeper significance when thought of as rejoicing in the actual presence of Hashem. Most significantly, we would need to revisit the various details and nuances we have highlighted in the particulars of this mitzvah and reexamine them specifically in their role of rejoicing *before God*. Each unique form of natural joy and its corresponding form of spiritual joy takes on a heightened and more vivid character when understood to be a component of a direct interaction with the Ultimate Source of all forms of joy and gladness.

The Mikdash

Though we have suggested that the words "before God" serve to define the very act of taking the species, they are also interpreted by the Sages to refer to the Mikdash. The full seven-day mitzvah of Arba Minim can be fulfilled only in the Mikdash.[7] Elsewhere, the obligation applies on only the first of the seven days of Sukkos. It is thus primarily a Mikdash related mitzvah.

This is well-understood in light of our suggestion that the presence of God is a necessary ingredient in this mitzvah. Though the state of standing before God can be achieved at some level in any location, it is only fully achieved in the Mikdash, the physical space in which Hashem's presence is fully manifested.

All three of the *Regalim* tie us to the Mikdash, the focal point of our existence. Yet the festival of Sukkos binds us to it even more, with its unique mitzvah that can be fulfilled only there.

---

7   The nature of the seven-day commandment in the Mikdash is not entirely clear. Some authorities take for granted that each individual is obligated to be in the Mikdash each day of Sukkos in order to take the species (*Netziv*, commentary to the *Sifri, Bamidbar* p. 270; Rav Y.P. Perlov, commentary to *Sefer HaMitzvos* of Rav Saadiah, vol. 3, chap. 5. See also *Mo'adim U'Zmanim*, 1:122 and footnote 1, who seems unsure about this). The more commonly accepted approach, however, seems to be that of the *Ritva* (*Sukkah* 43a) and the *Sefas Emes* (ibid. 41a), that only someone who finds himself in the Mikdash is obligated to take the species.

A Shift of Focus

As we have mentioned in an earlier chapter, the Biblical mitzvah of taking the Arba Minim (at least that mitzvah which applies even outside the Mikdash, on the first day of Sukkos) can be fulfilled only with specimens that actually belong to the person, but not borrowed specimens.

Yet according to the opinion of some major Rishonim, the unique obligation of taking the species in the Mikdash (for all seven days of Sukkos) may be fulfilled even with borrowed species.[8] They interpret the emphasis of "take for *yourself*" as referring solely to the immediately proximate clause of "take for yourself on the first day," but not the end of the verse which reads "and rejoice before God for seven days."

Earlier, we attempted to develop a theory of why one must own the specimens in order to discharge his obligation. We speculated that the unique nature of this mitzvah as one of using the species to rejoice before God requires a feeling of personal relationship that is possible only if one actually owns the samples.

If this approach is correct, we would need to explain why this should not hold true in the seven-day mitzvah that applies in the Mikdash. Why should the mitzvah of taking the species in the Mikdash be different?

We may speculate that there is a fundamental difference between the two parts of the mitzvah. On the first day of Sukkos, the rejoicing before God is performed on an individual basis. Each person on his own approaches God and rejoices before Him, with Him. Full experience of the species requires legal ownership over them.

On the subsequent days of Sukkos, those days on which the mitzvah is limited to the Mikdash, the nature of the mitzvah changes. The Mikdash is the entity that unites all of the Jewish People. During these days, the mitzvah is not for each individual to rejoice on his own before God, but for the Jewish People—as one entity—to experience and express its communal and collective joy. It is no longer necessary to own the species because the emphasis is no longer upon one's personal

---

8   See *Ramban, Milchamos Hashem*, beginning of the third chapter of *Sukkah*, as well as the *Ritva* to Sukkah 29b.

connection to God. Instead, the focus is upon the experience of rejoicing as one member of the greater community of Israel.[9]

Together, Before God

Perhaps there is another reason for the unique role played by unity in the application of this mitzvah in the Mikdash. As we suggested above, the mitzvah of the Arba Minim takes on a special quality in the Mikdash because of the unique role played by Hashem's process in this mitzvah. As we suggested, although the stance of "before God" can be created anywhere, it is more real, more authentic, when done in the actual place described as before God, where God's presence is more felt and more real.

It would seem that to stand in God's presence requires a connection greater than that available to one individual Jew on his own. Only as a unified whole can we actually "rejoice before God." The lower form of "before God," which applies anywhere, can be accessed by one individual, but the more actualized form of it cannot; hence the communal nature of that aspect of the mitzvah.

Klal Yisrael at the Summit

It is, once again, quite befitting that the mitzvah that stands at the summit of our spiritual strivings serve as one that unites all of the Jewish People as one entity. The ultimate relationship between the Jewish People and Hashem, after all, is that of the unified entity called Klal Yisrael relating to Hashem. It is only natural, then, that the point

---

9   This might explain the unusual nature of this mitzvah. As mentioned in the previous footnote, the mainstream approach seems to be that there is no obligation to be present in the Mikdash to perform the mitzvah of the Arba Minim there. Instead, the mitzvah only devolves upon someone who happens to be there. This is highly unusual. To the best of my knowledge, nowhere else do we find a mitzvah that only devolves upon someone if he happens to be in a specific place at a specific time. Based on the approach we have suggested, we could further suggest that the mitzvah of the Arba Minim in the Mikdash is one incumbent upon the entity of the Jewish People as a whole, not upon each individual. Although one is not obligated to be present in the Mikdash so as to take the Minim throughout the seven days of Sukkos, it might be incumbent upon the Jewish People as a whole to ensure that there are people present in the Mikdash performing this mitzvah. See *Ben Melech*, *Shemos* 12:47 who arrives at this conclusion.

of arrival be a mitzvah that is performed specifically as a member of that people, and not as a mere individual.

More on the Mikdash

We suggested that the focus on the Mikdash may have to do with the unique character of this mitzvah as requiring God's "Presence." Yet perhaps there is another factor at play here as well: As a mitzvah defined by rejoicing, it is best suited to the Mikdash, itself the ultimate source of joy. Throughout *Tanach*, we find Yerushalayim and the Mikdash being described as the place of happiness and joy. Again, in *Parashas Re'eh* we are enjoined to "go to the place that God has chosen...and rejoice there." And David HaMelech exclaims, "I rejoiced when people said to me, 'Let us go to the home of God.'"[10] Through the mitzvah of the Arba Minim, we connect to the unique joy of the Mikdash.

Indeed, this mitzvah stands apart from other mitzvos in its function of connecting us to the special joy experienced only in the Mikdash. Other Mikdash-related mitzvos, such as presenting oneself before God on the *Regalim*, focus not on the unique joy of the Mikdash, but on the fact that God's presence is primarily felt and found there. It is specifically the mitzvah of the Arba Minim that calls out to each one of us to come and participate in actively expressing the joy of standing before God in His Mikdash.

Intimations of Eternity

The festival of Sukkos, consummating as it does the cycle of the Jewish year, may provide us with context for all of our Divine service, as we have discussed. At the same time, it may provide us with a glimpse of the ultimate goal and objective of all that service.

The end-goal of creation is, as expressed by the Psalmist, "Let God's glory endure forever; Let God rejoice in His creations."[11]

Indeed, Sukkos is widely accepted to allude to *Olam Haba*, the ultimate world that will develop after the period of time during which we struggle to find ourselves and God in the darkness of this world.

---

10   *Tehillim* 122:1.
11   *Tehillim* 104:31.

As *Mesilas Yesharim* famously explains,[12] the purpose of creation is that man elevate not only himself, but the entirety of creation. This idea is perhaps expressed in the Lulav where, as we noted earlier, inanimate trees and plants join us in praising God.

The mitzvah of Lulav, as the epitome of rejoicing before God and, as we have suggested, *with* God, carries intimations of the ultimate goal and objective of creation.

Sukkah

Strictly speaking, there is no need to involve the mitzvah of sukkah in a discussion of Lulav. The two mitzvos, after all, are independent of each other, and in fact have no halachic connection. Yet it would be difficult to imagine that these two unrelated mitzvos happen to coincide with each other. And many people have incorporated into their fulfillment of the mitzvah of Lulav the teaching of the *Arizal* that the Arba Minim are to be taken specifically inside the sukkah.[13]

Is there anything to be said regarding the connection between Lulav and sukkah, within the context we have endeavored to create for understanding the mitzvah of the Arba Minim?

Based on what we have discovered in the previous chapter, there exists an obvious connection. Unlike most other mitzvos, the mitzvah of Lulav, by its very definition, is to be performed in the direct presence of God. The sukkah, of course, is to remind us of God's protection and presence. The Lulav cannot be taken just anywhere. Whether figuratively or literally, it requires a sukkah, a space consecrated by the tangible presence of Hashem before Whom we are to take up the species and rejoice.

---

12   Chap. 1.
13   Cited by the *Magen Avraham* 651:17.

CHAPTER 7

Wrapping It Up

Back in chapter one, we pointed out that the activities we are bidden to engage in during Sukkos, which serves as the culmination of the entire yearly cycle, can be presumed to speak to the sum total of our mission in life.

Having traversed the terrain of the mitzvah of the Arba Minim, let us revisit that thought.

If the Torah has defined the climax and culmination of the year as a time to rejoice before God with the species that elicit specific forms of joy, we need to contemplate what this tells us about the entirety of Torah. What context does this place all our Divine service into?

Avodas Hashem (serving God) is not fun and games. It can be difficult and demanding. It demands self-sacrifice. Yet by placing the mitzvah of the Arba Minim at the apex and culmination of the yearly cycle, the Torah has provided a certain context for all our work. It may be tough going, but the very knowledge that the end-goal is one of rejoicing before God puts all our striving into a different context.

There are three general levels in Divine service:

The first is spiritual sensitivity, awareness of those facets of oneself that need to be rectified.

The second is subduing one's natural desires and controlling them.

> The third is rectifying one's natural desires to the point that one is joyous and elated to serve God.
>
> *Rav Yisrael of Salant, Ohr Yisrael, n. 30 (paraphrased)*

Joy as an Ingredient

In summation of this section, let us take a step back and think about the mitzvah of the Arba Minim.

In a formula recited by many people before fulfilling a mitzvah, reference is made to fulfilling the mitzvah "along with all of the 613 mitzvos included in it." Rav Gedalia Schorr explained that each mitzvah introduces its own principle, its own mode of service, into our general Divine service.[1] Each and every mitzvah must be performed with all of these principles, but each principle has one mitzvah that is special for that principle, and that principle is the theme of that particular mitzvah. Any mitzvah, any act of Divine service, requires all aspects. Thus, every mitzvah must include the unique forms of *avodah* of all the other mitzvos.

As the Torah states clearly, the essence of the mitzvah of the Arba Minim is that of rejoicing before God. This is, of course, a central theme in all mitzvos. As the *Rambam* writes at the very end of *Hilchos Lulav*, "the joy felt at performing a mitzvah is a great component of Divine service."

Within the mitzvah of the Arba Minim, then, the concept of experiencing joy in serving God is crystallized into a specific mitzvah of its own. While the joy of serving God is a crucial component in all mitzvos, when it comes to the Arba Minim, it is the very essence of the mitzvah itself. It is the mitzvah of the Arba Minim that trains us to practice this joy. And through proper fulfillment of this mitzvah, we develop the ability to incorporate this ingredient into the performance of all the other mitzvos.[2]

---

1   *Ohr Gedalyahu, Behar*, p. 69.

2   It is no coincidence that the *Rambam's* seminal proclamation about the centrality of joy in

עִיקָר עֲשִׂיַּת הַמִּצְוָה הוּא שִׂמְחָתָה שֶׁזָּכִינוּ לְכָךְ.

The most central aspect of a mitzvah is joy over the fact that we merit to perform it.

Chazon Ish, Collected Letters, vol. 2, no. 93

Integrating joy into our mitzvos, however, is only the beginning. If our hypothesis is correct—namely, that the Torah has designed the Arba Minim to evoke and express four distinct forms of natural joy, each with a corresponding form of spiritual joy—we would need to learn how to incorporate each of these forms of joy into each of our mitzvos.

Taking the Esrog would train us to relate to the grandeur of He Who has commanded us on each of the mitzvos. It would teach us to focus on the nobility conferred upon ourselves by performing these mitzvos and interacting with the greatness of God. It would help us learn to experience the joy engendered by being in the presence of, and attaining, true nobility and majesty.

By taking the Lulav, with the exuberant joy it expresses, we would educate ourselves to sense this exuberant joy in every interaction with Hashem, His Torah, and His mitzvos.

The Hadassim sensitize us to notice and take joy in the complexity, symmetry, and beauty of each of the mitzvos.

The Aravos bring us to the life-giving, joyful nature of each and every mitzvah.

Truly, each mitzvah can be performed in an Esrog-like manner, in a Lulav-like manner, and so on; and ideally, in such a manner that incorporates each of the Minim. Each of the Minim spreads out far beyond itself in its message and impact.

---

serving Hashem serves as the closing statement of *Hilchos Lulav*, working off the very same verse that gives us the mitzvah of the Arba Minim.

A Very Human Mitzvah

A question we may harbor, consciously or otherwise, is, "does the Torah communicate with us as human beings? Can we, in all of our humanity, connect fully to the Torah?"

In the mitzvah of the Arba Minim we discover that it is precisely as human beings, with everything that this entails, that we approach Hashem and serve Him. This mitzvah does not ask of us to put our humanity aside and serve God from a point of transcendence. To the contrary! It calls upon us to activate our most subtle sensitivities for the sake of creating a richer and fuller relationship with the Divine.

In general, if we are understanding the mitzvah of Lulav correctly, this mitzvah should inform us that the Torah is speaking to human beings who are in tune with their surroundings, who are sensitive to the world around them and everything contained in it. The Torah expects us to be not only people whose aesthetic sensibilities are easily awakened, but whose psyches know precisely how to catalog and what to do with the stimuli. Torah speaks to the organic, natural man, not the artificial, synthetic, sterile man.

Indeed, the mitzvah itself tells us about the type of person the Torah expects us to be. This is included in the education each mitzvah affords us. Not only does actually carrying out the mitzvah educate us toward certain values, but even contemplating the psychological prerequisites of the mitzvah teaches us about the Torah's vision for human beings.

CHAPTER 8

Midrashic Interpretations
God, Israel, and the Totality of Man

As we noted in the opening chapter, the Midrash offers numerous symbolisms of the Arba Minim. As we suggested there, the Midrash does not intend to say that this is the essential meaning of the mitzvah, but to build additional levels of depth on top of the simple meaning.

Let us examine three of the most well-known ideas mentioned by the Midrash and contemplate how each of these interpretations builds on the core concepts we have tried to elucidate:[1]

- Each of the Arba Minim can be linked symbolically to God.[2] The Arba Minim are all used to rejoice before Hashem. It is therefore appropriate to utilize in our praise and thanksgiving to Hashem, items that can all be seen as alluding to the greatness of Hashem Himself.

- The species symbolize the various members of the Jewish People.[3] We use the Arba Minim to celebrate the unique relationship between the Jewish People and God, and so it is appropriate that they allude to the members of Klal Yisrael, the nation selected to have a unique relationship with Hashem. More significantly,

---

1   Based on *sefer Ben Melech*, p. 66.
2   *Vayikra Rabbah* 30:9.
3   Ibid., 12.

the joy is only complete when it is all of Yisrael together. We recognize the need for the inclusion of all sectors of the Jewish People in our rejoicing over being God's chosen nation.

- The species represent the various central organs of the human body.[4] The species are used to recite *Hallel* and praise God, which should be done with the entirety of one's personality; this is expressed by using species that can be associated with the organs used to praise Hashem.

All of these become meaningful only once we understand the essence of what it is that we are doing with the species, which is rejoicing before God.

Weapons

One of the Midrashic interpretations of the meaning of the Arba Minim is as *manin d'krav* (weapons).[5] The Midrash sees the taking of the species as an exultant expression of our having emerged victorious from the judgment of Rosh Hashanah, during which we were pitted against the nations of the world.

In a similar vein, the Gemara relates that one of the great Sages, upon shaking his Lulav, would exclaim: "This is an arrow in the eye of the Satan!"[6] The Gemara counsels against actually saying this, but the message is clear: The Lulav can be looked at metaphorically as a spear with which to attack the forces of evil in the world.

If the species are all about rejoicing, how does this connect to weaponry and thrusting the Lulav into the Satan's eye?

Apparently, our weapon against the forces which wish to uproot us is the joy we experience and express in the presence of God and over our relationship with Him. It is one thing to observe mitzvos; it is an entirely different matter to develop a connection to our mitzvah observance to the point that we can truly find joy in it. The expression of joy in *avodas Hashem* is indeed an arrow in the eyes of the Satan,

---

4   Ibid., 14.
5   Ibid., 2.
6   *Sukkah* 38a.

because once mitzvos are practiced not out of compulsion but willingly and joyfully, he does not stand a chance.

On a related note, the Gemara explains that the reason for waving the species back and forth and up and down is to prevent evil spirits and to stop harmful winds and dew. How does that fit with our claim, taken directly from the Rishonim—and clearly manifested from the fact that we do this while thanking Hashem during *Hallel*—that waving the species is done as an expression of joy?

In actuality, it needs to be understood how waving the species is supposed to protect us in the first place.

Some suggest, somewhat homiletically, that it is the very joy expressed by waving the species that protects us from harmful influences.[7]

Truthfully, however, it would appear that the Gemara's statements about protecting ourselves by waving the species contain secrets that go deeper than the simple, basic approach we have attempted to formulate in understanding the nature of this mitzvah.

---

7   *Peninei Rabbeinu Yechezkel* (citing Rav Yechezkel Abramski), p. 56; *Gevuros Yitzchak, Sukkos* 23.

Hadar Reclaimed

CHAPTER 9

The Hadar Factor

In section one, we explored the essence of the mitzvah of the Arba Minim as described by the Torah—that of rejoicing before God. At this point we turn our attention to another concept that plays a prominent role in this mitzvah—that of *hadar*.[1]

The Esrog is characterized by the Torah as "the fruit of a *hadar* tree," and the Oral Torah explains that in fact all four of the species must meet the criterion of *hadar*. Earlier, we explored the meaning of *hadar* as well as the prominent role it plays in this mitzvah. In that discussion, we took the approach that *hadar* is important primarily as a means of facilitating joy, and more specifically, facilitating a specific type of joy. According to that approach, it is not *hadar* per se that the Torah calls for, but the particular form of joy inspired by *hadar*.

While the idea of incorporating *hadar* within the core definition of this mitzvah—that of rejoicing—is undoubtedly true, there would seem to be evidence that the function and role of *hadar* in this mitzvah goes deeper than that.

First, it seems difficult to ignore the fact that, whatever the underlying reason, the Torah has essentially placed *hadar* at the focal point of the Jewish year. Even assuming that *hadar* is subservient to a more

---

1   Throughout this section, we will be using the term "beauty" in conjunction with *hadar*. As previously discussed, *hadar* refers to a very specific form of beauty: one tinged with grandeur and majesty; and it is in this sense that we use the term beauty in the context of this section as well.

prominently featured concept—that of rejoicing before Hashem—the fact is that the Torah has us focusing all our attentions on the concept of *hadar*. Think of the days and weeks leading up to Sukkos: Seemingly rational people can be found agonizing over whether a certain fruit is or is not blemished, or whether a given palm frond is nicked at its tip in such a way that it would forfeit its *hadar* status. It is difficult to regard this atmosphere as coincidental. It simply cannot be denied that on a practical level, the Torah has made Sukkos, the summit of the spiritual year, revolve around the concept of *hadar*.

Sukkos in Summation

That *hadar* plays an intrinsic role in the mitzvah of the Arba Minim is borne out by a comment of the Vilna Gaon. Commenting on the verse in *Eishes Chayil*,[2] "Her vestments are *oz* (strength) and *hadar*, and she laughs on the last day," the Gaon writes:

> Her vestments are strength and hadar. Strength—this refers to the days of Judgment, Rosh Hashanah and Yom Kippur. Hadar—this refers to Sukkos, when we take the pri eitz hadar. And she laughs on the last day—this refers to Shemini Atzeres, concerning which it is written, "You shall be only joyous."

It is obvious that the Gaon sees the concept of *hadar* as actually descriptive of the entirety of Sukkos. Clearly, then, *hadar* goes beyond simply facilitating a certain type of joy, and instead, takes on a life of its own.

Show Me Your Beauty

A statement of the Midrash brings home further the idea that the beauty of the Arba Minim is central to the mitzvah. Commenting on God's words to Israel (*Shir Hashirim* 2:14), "Show me your appearance...for your appearance is comely," the Midrash (*Yalkut Shimoni*, ibid., 986) explains: "Show Me your appearance—with a beautiful Lulav and Esrog." Here, again, we have the Midrash isolating the beauty of the

---

2   *Mishlei* 31:25.

Arba Minim as inherently significant, going beyond their joy-inducing properties.[3]

What is it about *hadar* that is so significant that causes it to take a place of prominence as the center of all our strivings?

More acutely: What message does the Torah seek to impart to us by positioning *hadar* at the summit of our journey? These are the questions that we must attempt to address in this section.

The *Hiddur Mitzvah* Connection

In order to better understand the centrality of *hadar*, we need to examine its relationship with its close relative, the concept of *hiddur mitzvah*.

Hiddur mitzvah is a concept that applies to all mitzvos.[4] Every mitzvah should be performed in the most beautiful way. At the simplest level, this means that the object used for the mitzvah must be beautiful. As the Gemara states, one should "make a beautiful shofar, a beautiful tallis, a beautiful *Sefer Torah*, etc."[5]

If all mitzvos require *hiddur*, in what way is the *hadar* of the Arba Minim unique?

Two factors distinguish the *hadar* requirement from all other mitzvos.

First, the Torah has included the need for *hadar* in the definition of the mitzvah itself. Unlike *hiddur mitzvah*, which does not define the essence of any given mitzvah, the concept of *hadar* is not only integral to, but definitive of, the very essence of the mitzvah of the Arba Minim—certainly the Esrog.

Second—and as a direct corollary of the first factor—although there is certainly a mitzvah to beautify any mitzvah object, a lack of *hiddur* generally does not disqualify an item from being used for a mitzvah. When it comes to the Arba Minim, on the other hand, lack of *hadar* indeed disqualifies the Minim.[6]

It thus emerges that the obligation to take a beautiful Esrog does not stem from the general obligation of *hiddur mitzvah*, but rather, from

---

3 More on this Midrash in a later chapter.
4 *Shabbos* 133b; *Bava Kama* 9b.
5 *Shabbos* ad loc.
6 See *Tosafos, Sukkah* 29b s.v. *ba'inan*, who explains this distinction.

the unique concept of *hadar* expressed specifically by the Torah in the context of the Arba Minim.

This is not to say that there is no connection between the general concept of *hiddur Mitzvah* and the unique *hadar* of the Arba Minim. To the extent that the *hadar* of the Minim has inherent significance, it emerges that it is the same concept as that of *hiddur mitzvah*—only with a much more prominent role. The very same *hiddur* that hovers over every mitzvah, playing a seemingly peripheral role but not becoming part of its essence, reappears within the mitzvah of the Arba Minim as a seminal feature of the mitzvah, without which the mitzvah is inherently incomplete.[7]

Put differently, the general principle of *hiddur mitzvah* is crystallized into one specific mitzvah whose very essence is that of *hiddur*.[8]

Not only, though, has the Torah crystallized the concept of *hiddur mitzvah* into one particular mitzvah, it has positioned that mitzvah at the apex of our spiritual strivings.

If this is correct, then a prerequisite to gaining a deeper understanding of the essence of the Arba Minim is gaining insight into the nature of *hiddur mitzvah* itself. Only after properly understanding the concept of *hiddur mitzvah* can we understand the essence of the mitzvah of the Arba Minim, which is a concerted focus on the idea of *hiddur mitzvah*.

---

7   *Rashi* (*Sukkah* ibid.) makes this connection extremely clear. According to *Rashi*, as explained
      by the *Chiddushei HaGriz* in *Nazir* 2b; *Harerei Kedem* 1:124; *Kuntres HaBiurim, Sukkah* 22:5,
      the Torah's presentation of the word *hadar* simply informs us that the general concept of
      hiddur mitzvah becomes crucial to the mitzvah of the Arba Minim.

8   In the first section we cited the explanation of Rav Gedalia Schorr that each mitzvah con-
      tains a specific principle that must then be incorporated into the performance of all other
      mitzvos. In our context, this would mean that *hiddur mitzvah* is the underlying theme of the
      Arba Minim and is then applied to every other mitzvah.

CHAPTER 10

The Essence of Hiddur Mitzvah

What is *hiddur mitzvah* all about?

Why does God care what my tallis looks like? Shouldn't we be focused on the spiritual nature of things to the point that the aesthetic appearance of our mitzvah items makes no difference to us? Does it really matter whether my shofar is a beautiful one or not?

At a simple level, *hiddur mitzvah* is a way of giving honor to the mitzvos and, by extension, to the One Who has commanded us with them.[1] Since we function within a physical world, it is necessary for us to express our reverence and love for the mitzvos in a way that is meaningful to us as physical beings; this is accomplished by beautifying the mitzvos.

Hiddur mitzvah also demonstrates a deep love for the mitzvos. It shows that we are not performing them out of rote but, instead, cherish and value them.

These ideas are certainly true, and it is possible that at a purely halachic level, showing a display of honor and fondness for the mitzvos is indeed the definition of and motivation behind *hiddur mitzvah*. However, upon

---

1   See *Ritva, Shevuos* 16a, as well as *Mesilas Yesharim* chap. 19.

examination of the source for this concept in the Torah, it would seem that we are pointed toward something more profound than this.

Hiddur mitzvah is derived from the verse that states, "This is my God, and I will beautify Him."[2] The Sages explain that going beyond the simple meaning of "I will beautify Him," the word *ve'anveihu* can also be read as "I will beautify myself before Him."

A careful reading of this verse, as interpreted by the Sages, tells us that with *hiddur mitzvah*, it is not only the mitzvah that we are "adorning;" it is primarily about adorning *ourselves*![3]

Moreover, the verse makes absolutely no mention of mitzvos. It speaks only about beautifying ourselves. If the root of this concept is that of displaying honor for the mitzvos, it would emerge that the verse has left out the most important part of the equation, namely the mitzvos themselves. Instead, it would seem as if beautifying ourselves has inherent significance and just happens to be accomplished through beautifying the mitzvos.[4]

Furthermore, the Sages speak not simply about "beautifying oneself" with the mitzvos, but about "beautifying oneself *before God*."

What is this all about? What is the vision of beautifying oneself before God, and how does performing mitzvos in an aesthetically pleasing manner beautify the person performing them?

The Beauty of Mitzvos

The mitzvos are designed to elevate and ennoble us. Each mitzvah has its own unique character, its own underlying principle or principles; each mitzvah beautifies the person performing it in its unique way. Each mitzvah addresses a different part of our psyche and character, guiding us in beautifying that particular aspect of ourselves. Through performing each and every mitzvah properly, one achieves true spiritual beauty.

---

2   *Shemos* 15:2.

3   The idea that *hiddur mitzvah* is a beautification of one's self has halachic ramifications; see *Nazir* 2b.

4   It is also worth noting that, with some exceptions, the mitzvos had not even been given to the Jewish people at the time this declaration was uttered; it was before the giving of the Torah.

We might take for granted many of the mitzvos we perform on a regular basis. Consider, though, a handful of those mitzvos. What would we be like without them? What would we look like as individuals, and what would the Jewish People look like as a nation, without the mitzvah of Shabbos? Without the mitzvah to "love your fellow like yourself?" Without the mitzvos of *Birkas Hamazon*, eating matzoh on Pesach, laying tefillin, or reciting the *Shema*?

There can be little doubt that the mitzvos, performed with the proper understanding, attention, and approach, confer beauty upon each of us individually and on the entity of the Jewish People as a whole.

Expressing the Beauty

How can a mitzvah be performed in a way that expresses the attainment of beauty and appreciation of that beauty? What is the difference between a mitzvah performed simply as a matter of rote, or even as a way of discharging one's obligation, and a mitzvah performed in the spirit of attaining spiritual beauty?

The answer is, of course, *hiddur mitzvah*. By physically beautifying our mitzvah items, we demonstrate—and allow ourselves to internalize—our awareness of the beauty of the mitzvah itself, as well as the beauty it confers upon us. The aesthetic beauty incorporated into the performance of the mitzvah is designed to evoke and express the beauty that is inherent in the mitzvah itself. I adorn myself, so to speak, with a beautiful shofar, to express the spiritual beauty with which I adorn myself by performing the mitzvah of shofar itself. I beautify my tallis to demonstrate the beauty the mitzvah of tzitzis brings to my personality and soul. The aesthetic beauty that I add to my performance of the mitzvah is merely an expression of the underlying, inherent beauty of the mitzvah itself.

Dual Meaning

Let's reread the words of the Sages, "I will beautify myself before Him with mitzvos." If we listen carefully, it sounds as if the mitzvos themselves, sans any artificial beautification, are making us beautiful. But then the Sages go on to talk about using a beautiful shofar! Perhaps that is exactly the point, and the phrase has a double meaning. The first and deeper meaning is, I will beautify myself before Him by performing mitzvos that inherently are beautiful. The second level is, I will give physical expression to this beauty by performing mitzvos in an aesthetically pleasing manner.

Hiddur mitzvah is the physical manifestation of the spiritual beauty of the mitzvah itself. Since we are physical beings, the Torah mandates that the spiritual beauty of the mitzvos take on a physical expression. This is accomplished by ensuring that the items we use for the mitzvos are beautiful.

Paradigm Shift

If our understanding of the concept of *hiddur mitzvah* is correct, the underlying concept itself—the mitzvos as an attempt to beautify ourselves, individually and collectively—brings added levels of meaning to our performance of the mitzvos.

Of course, there are many sources that support this perspective. One is *Mishlei* (1:9): "For they are an ornament of grace upon your head, and a chain to adorn your neck." As explained by the Vilna Gaon, "The Torah and mitzvos are themselves adornments to the head and the body."[5]

Indeed, the entirety of *Shir Hashirim* revolves around God's repeated declarations of the beauty of Israel, His "beloved," all of which are explained by Chazal and the commentaries as referring to the beauty achieved by the actions and qualities of the Jewish People.[6]

יסוד לנפש האדם וצבי עדיו, והטוב והעיקר והתועלת והיקר אשר בו, עבודת השם
יתברך ויראתו ותורתו.

The very foundation of man's soul; its beauty; its goodness, main purpose, and glory, is that of serving God, fearing Him, and following His Torah.

Rabbeinu Yonah, Shaarei Teshuvah 3:148

---

5   See also *Rashi* to that verse.
6   We will return to this later with a reference to the mitzvah of the Arba Minim in *Shir Hashirim*.

Hiddur at the Center

We have formulated an understanding of *hiddur mitzvah*, but more work needs to be done before we can grasp just how central *hiddur mitzvah* is to our mission.

Unlike most mitzvos and obligations, the requirement of *hiddur mitzvah* is not stated as a command. Instead, it is derived from a proclamation made by the Jewish People themselves. As mentioned above, the source for this concept is the declaration, "This is my God, and I will beautify Him." In order to properly understand the implications of *hiddur mitzvah*, we need to revisit the moment of our acceptance and declaration of it as a mission.

Let's review the context of this verse. This dramatic declaration was among the first words articulated by the Jewish People after seeing the miracles that had been done for them.

The verse can be broken down into two parts. Each includes an exclamation and then a declaration of intent for the future:

- "This is my God—and I will beautify Him."
- "[This is] the God of my father—and I will uplift Him."

Aside from simply having been saved, the Jewish People were witness to unprecedented Divine revelations at the Sea. The revelation of God's glory that they were privy to prompted them to exclaim: "This is my God!" As the Sages point out, these words imply a sense of immediacy and intimacy. In their words, "We learn from this wording that each person was able to point with his finger at God." Moreover, so vivid was their perception, so great the revelation, that they were able to speak about it in terms usually reserved for something concrete and tangible.

It is from the immediacy of the words, "This is my God!" that the Sages derived the well-known teaching that a maidservant present at the splitting of the sea saw more [of God's glory] than the Navi Yechezkel.[7]

---

7   *Mechilta. Rashi* paraphrases this: "This is my God—[Hashem] revealed Himself to them in His glory, and each person was able to point with his or her finger."

In the same breath, the Jewish People continued by declaring, "I will beautify Him—this is my God, and [therefore] I will beautify Him." It is clear their pledge to "beautify" God was a direct, immediate, and perhaps almost intuitive reaction to the experience of having encountered God. "I have come so close to God that I can physically point at Him; therefore, I will beautify Him."

As explained by the Sages, "I will beautify Him" means I will beautify myself before Him with mitzvos, which essentially means, I will make a beautiful shofar, beautiful tallis, etc. This seems astonishing. The Jewish People have come face to face, as it were, with God, for the very first time. The experience affects them so powerfully that they are moved to express their commitment to venerating God. What form does this commitment take? Not, "I will spend my life adhering to His commandments," and not even, "I will give my life for Him," but "I will make sure my shofar is nice looking!" How does this purport to capture the essence of what we aspire to?

Compare this declaration to another interpretation given by the Sages to the words "I will beautify Him": "I will relate His beauty to the rest of the world."[8] This seems reasonable. A natural response to encountering the beauty and splendor of God is a desire to "tell it to the world." This seems closer to what we would see as definitive of a mission they would embrace upon encountering God. (In fact, this is the interpretation cited by *Rashi*, presumably because it is more straightforward, closer to the simple meaning of the text, and more easily understood based on the context.)

How, by contrast, does "I will beautify myself before Him with mitzvos" compare as a mission statement, or at least as a reaction of the Jewish People's first-time encounter with God? What is the relationship between the revelations the Jewish People were privy to and their reaction, which is captured by the concept of using beautiful mitzvah items?

---

8   *Mechilta* to this verse.

Encounter with Transcendent Beauty

To better understand the declaration of "I will beautify myself," we need to think more about what it was the Jewish People apprehended when God "revealed" Himself to them. What does one "see" upon encountering God?

We obviously cannot comprehend the revelations to which they were privy. However, we do know that what they had encountered was the ineffable beauty, majesty, and splendor of God. Of course, we cannot describe God's essence in any way, even if only metaphorically. The beauty and splendor we speak of emanate from God's essence but do not in any way define it. And of course, this refers not to any physical beauty, but to a spiritual, transcendent beauty that in fact eclipses—and is the very source of—any beauty we have ever come into contact with.

We may often think of God in other terms, but the concept of God's beauty and splendor is firmly rooted in Torah sources. *Shir Hashirim*, the love song between the Jewish People and God, is full of metaphorical praises of God's beauty, as it were. We are told that the ultimate delight—the reward attained only in the next world—is that of "basking in the splendor of the Divine presence." The Hebrew word used in this statement, *ziv*, is usually translated as "shine" or "radiance," and indeed is clearly used sometimes in that context. In fact, *ziv* is the Aramaic translation of *hadar*, which is closer to "beauty" or "splendor." Clearly, God's beauty and splendor are enough to gladden us for all eternity. In the words of the poem *Yedid Nefesh*, God is "the resplendent One, the beautiful One, Radiance of the universe."

The central feature of God's revelation to the Jewish People was His beauty and splendor, which is borne out by the other interpretation to the words "I will beautify Him," which we viewed above, "I will relate His beauty to the world." Clearly, it was their conception of God's grandeur and beauty that moved them the most.

Response

What is our reaction upon coming face to face with breathtaking beauty? The natural response is to wish to somehow be worthy of that beauty. We wish we had it for ourselves. We might feel impoverished and unworthy in its face, and search desperately for a way to claim some of it as our own.

The Jewish People have come face to face, so to speak, with the ineffable greatness of God, the source of all beauty and grandeur. This inspires within them a powerful reaction. One possible reaction would be a desire to proclaim God's "beauty" to the entire world. According to the interpretation of "I will beautify myself before Him with mitzvos," their reaction is the desire to reflect that beauty. They want to be able to be worthy of an association with it. Perhaps they even want to be able to be vehicles to express that beauty in the world. God's "beauty," of course, is not a physical one; it can best be approximated by attaining spiritual and ethical beauty. They intuitively understand that this can be achieved through the mitzvos, the divine commands that contain within them the secrets to attaining something of the beauty and splendor of God that they had glimpsed. This, in turn, is best expressed physically by performing those mitzvos in a physically beautiful manner.

"I will beautify myself before Him by making a beautiful shofar, lulav, tallis etc.," in actuality means, I have encountered the beauty of God to the point that I was able to point and say, 'This is my God!' I pledge to use God's commandments to beautify myself so that I can attain some of that beauty myself. I will express this in a concrete way by physically beautifying the mitzvah objects, thus expressing my awareness and appreciation for the beauty and majesty attainable through the mitzvos themselves.

Reflecting Back

Earlier, we formulated the idea that the purpose of *hiddur mitzvah* is that of expressing the inherent beauty of the mitzvah itself, which is conferred upon the person performing it. Based on our examination of the original context of the catalyst of *hiddur mitzvah*, we must add to this. *Hiddur mitzvah* goes beyond expressing to ourselves the beauty attained through each mitzvah. With *hiddur mitzvah*, we present ourselves before God, the source of beauty and splendor, and attempt to somehow mirror His beauty through the performance of the mitzvah and the physical expression of the beauty we achieve in doing so.

Hiddur mitzvah, then, brings us back to that initial moment of encounter with the beauty and splendor of Hashem. It captures our reaction to that encounter and translates it into an understanding of the beauty and splendor contained within the mitzvos, affording us the opportunity to reflect back a spark of that beauty and splendor.

זה א-לי ואנוהו—אתנאה לפניו במצוות: יסוד הדורם של מצוות הוא בהכרת נאותו של הקב"ה, והוא הפירוש ב"אתנאה לפניו."

The basis of *hiddur mitzvah* is the recognition of the beauty of God. This is the meaning of "I will beautify myself before Him"—I will beautify myself before Him with mitzvos.

Rav Yechezkel Sarna, Dalios Yechezkel 1, p. 200

CHAPTER 11

Show Me Your Appearance

Having formulated a deeper understanding of the concept of *hiddur mitzvah*, we can now revisit the connection between the general concept of *hiddur mitzvah* on the one hand, and *hadar* of the Arba Minim on the other.

As we observed, with regard to *hiddur mitzvah*, it is not so much about beautifying the mitzvos as it is about beautifying ourselves by beautifying the mitzvos. If our hypothesis about the *hadar* of the Arba Minim as a crystallization of *hiddur mitzvah* is correct, we should expect to discover that the same is true about the Arba Minim. Is this true? Are we somehow draping ourselves with *hadar* when we take the Esrog and the other species?

Let us take a better look at the Vilna Gaon's explanation of "*Oz ve'hadar levushah*." As the Gaon explains, the "woman of valor" being depicted by that section of *Mishlei* is the entity of Klal Yisrael, the Jewish People. The verse describes the "garments" of the Jewish People, one of which is *hadar*. If we listen carefully, it is saying that the Jewish People *dresses itself in hadar* on Sukkos." Clearly, through the mitzvah of the Arba Minim, the Jewish People, as a whole, are adorning themselves with hadar.

Adorning Ourselves with the Species

This is made even more clear by the Midrash we viewed above, "Show Me your appearance—by taking a beautiful Esrog and Lulav." This is strange. Who is beautiful here—the Esrog, or the person taking it?

114

How does holding a beautiful Esrog answer God's call of "Show Me your appearance...for your appearance is comely?"

Evidently, the Minim are not something external to us that we engage with. The act of taking the Minim is one of adorning ourselves with beauty and *hadar*. In taking the species, all of which possess the quality of *hadar*, we make ourselves "beautiful."

It is manifestly clear that just as *hiddur mitzvah* in general serves to "beautify" the person before God, the Arba Minim do the same.

As we explained earlier, the *hiddur mitzvah* attendant to any given mitzvah serves to express the specific spiritual beauty achieved by the person performing that mitzvah. With the Arba Minim, though, the *hadar* is not attendant to the mitzvah but, instead, forms its essence. What, then, is the unique spiritual beauty being expressed by the *hadar* of the Arba Minim?

It would seem that the *hadar* of the Arba Minim serves to express the beauty attained *through the sum total of all a person's mitzvos together*.

To the extent that the *hadar* of the Arba Minim is a crystallization of the general concept of *hiddur mitzvah*, the spiritual beauty expressed through it is a crystallization of the beauty attained by all our Divine service.

The physical *hadar* of the Arba Minim is to the general beauty attained through mitzvos, what the *hiddur mitzvah* of a given mitzvah is to the specific spiritual beauty attained through that mitzvah.

The qualitative difference between the beautification of *hiddur mitzvah* and that of the Arba Minim is evident in the very act of the mitzvah of the Minim. Although *hiddur mitzvah* serves to "beautify" the person performing the mitzvah, this cannot be seen in a literal manner, as the mitzvah does not necessarily serve as an adornment. For example, a person reading from a beautiful *Sefer Torah* does not use the *Sefer Torah* to physically adorn himself. The adornment with the *hiddur* of the *Sefer Torah* is somewhat removed from his physical body.

Not so with the Arba Minim. "Taking" the Arba Minim is quite literally an act of adorning one's person with them. "Take" the *hadar* of the Minim and adorn yourself with it, and in so doing, express the *hiddur* you have attained through all your mitzvos and Divine service.

When *Mishlei* speaks of the Jewish People as "dressing itself in *hadar*," it refers not only to the physical act of holding the Esrog, but to the underlying *hadar* achieved by the Jewish People; a *hadar* fully attained and then expressed on Sukkos through the physical mitzvah of taking the Arba Minim.

"Show Me your appearance," as interpreted by the Midrash, means to show Me the beauty you have attained through all of your mitzvos, expressed physically through the act of adorning yourself with a beautiful Esrog and Lulav.[1]

Hadar Accomplished

Having understood the significance and centrality of *hiddur mitzvah*, we are now better equipped to understand the centrality of the mitzvah of the Arba Minim which, as we have suggested, is an embodiment of the concept of *hiddur mitzvah*.

Earlier, we asked why *hiddur mitzvah* is so important that the mitzvah that embodies it is placed at the apex of the spiritual cycle. As we saw before, the Jewish People speak about *hiddur mitzvah* in terms clearly implying that this concept captures the essence of our mission. It should come as no surprise that the mitzvah positioned at the point of arrival, so to speak, where we have completed our mission for that year, should be patterned specifically around *hiddur mitzvah*.

Throughout the year, we strive to beautify ourselves one mitzvah at a time, expressing this beautification through *hiddur mitzvah*. On Sukkos we arrive at our destination. We achieve the right to physically demonstrate our hard-earned *hadar* by adorning ourselves with the Arba Minim.[2]

---

1   In fact, this interpretation of the Midrash—that the *hadar* of the Esrog and Lulav express the innate beauty achieved by the Jewish People—seems compelling based on the context. God's call to "Show Me your appearance, let Me hear your voice," is a general declaration. Nothing about it or its context would suggest that it refers specifically to Sukkos or the Arba Minim. How, then, can it be interpreted as referring to a specific mitzvah done at a specific time? It seems clear that the Arba Minim are indeed used to "show" God one's innate beauty, which in turn is the cumulative effect of all of one's spiritual strivings.

2   In truth, the concept of showing our beauty before God is manifest during each of the three

Our mission statement—"I will beautify myself before God by performing the mitzvos, expressed through *hiddur mitzvah*"—comes to full fruition on Sukkos, when God tells us, "Show Me your appearance, for your appearance is comely—as expressed through a beautiful Esrog and Lulav."[3]

Regalim. The mitzvah of entering the Mikdash on the *Shalosh Regalim* requires us to "be seen before God." What is this all about? What exactly are we showing God?

The Midrash (*Shir Hashirim* 2) explains that this mitzvah is referred to by God when He says, "Show Me your appearance...for your appearance is comely." God commands us to come before Him to display our beauty. This is true of all *Regalim*, but it is on Sukkos—the culmination of the three *Regalim*—that it comes to full fruition and is even expressed physically with the Arba Minim.

3　　At a deeper level, the mission of beautifying ourselves before God is that of reclaiming the splendor and beauty that originally belonged to Adam HaRishon. Adam was originally created with immense beauty and splendor. In fact, the Gemara (*Bava Metzia* 84a) specifically uses the word *hadar* in this context. As the Psalmist writes, "You have crowned Him with glory and splendor (*hadar*)." The *Maharal* explains, "Man was created in the Image of God; therefore, his face had *hadar* and beauty. This was the light that shone forth from the face of Adam..."

When Adam sinned, he lost this, together with many other things. The Midrash states (*Bereishis Rabbah* 12:6): Adam lost six commodities when he sinned, one of which was the *ziv* (splendor) of his face. (*Ziv* is the Aramaic word for *hadar*; see Onkelos to *Devarim* 33:17). When the Jewish People come face to face with Hashem at *K'rias Yam Suf*, perceiving His beauty, which they sense should be reflected in themselves, they recognize that their mission is that of reclaiming that lost beauty and *hadar* through mitzvos, expressed through *hiddur mitzvah* and ultimately through the mitzvah of the Arba Minim. (It is perhaps no coincidence that the Esrog represents a rectification of the sin of the Tree of Knowledge.) "I will beautify myself before Him"—I will reclaim the beauty and *hadar* that is humanity's birthright.

CHAPTER 12

Back to the Basics

In the first section of this book, we focused on some of the particulars of the mitzvah of the Arba Minim and how they relate to the underlying theme of the mitzvah. In that context, the focus was on the theme of joy and *simchah*. Having focused in this section on the concept of *hadar*, let us reexamine some of those laws within the context of *hadar*.

Taking

The Torah instructs us to "take" the Arba Minim—that is, to physically take them in hand. As is evident from the Midrash, one of the meanings behind this is to "adorn" oneself with the Minim. By picking up and holding the Minim, we are taking from their *hadar* and incorporating it within our persona, both literally and figuratively.

Waving

The Minim are to be waved around. Perhaps this is an act of displaying our *hadar* before God.

Yours

The species must belong to the person taking them. Perhaps this reflects the need to "make the *hadar* our own," to bring it into ourselves.

Before God

The mitzvah of the Arba Minim is performed in the presence of God, so to speak. As we saw above, the essence of *hiddur mitzvah*, as well as that of *hadar*, is that of "beautifying oneself *before God.*" The essence of *hiddur mitzvah* is that of displaying my *hiddur* to God, so it certainly requires His presence. In the words of the Midrash, God asks us to "show Him our beauty" with a beautiful Esrog! Clearly, the whole point is to display our *hadar* before God, something which is impossible without the presence, so to speak, of God.

Impact

In the first section of this book, we focused on the core essence of the mitzvah of the Arba Minim: rejoicing before God, with everything that entails. The mitzvah of experiencing joy deals with a subjective emotional state. We are commanded to take certain actions to elicit that state.

In this section we have sought to demonstrate that the mitzvah goes beyond the subjective and says something about our objective state of affairs. It taps into something about who we are and have become throughout the year. The mitzvah itself, at this level, does its work irrespective of how we may happen to feel about it. It brings out the intrinsic *hadar* we have created within ourselves. At the same time, awareness of what we are doing with the Minim forces us to get in touch, on a personal, subjective level, with what we have really been doing with all of our mitzvos. Our subjective awareness of the objective reality of what we are doing can have a profound effect on us and our *avodah*.

Looking Backward

Our encounter with *hiddur mitzvah* at the summit of our annual spiritual pilgrimage forces us to look backward and see our strivings and accomplishments as a striving toward spiritual beauty. The potential for beauty is latent within our mitzvos, but we may not have tapped them for that potential. The Arba Minim experience allows us to go back and mine them for the *hadar* contained within them.

Looking Ahead

But it is not only the experience of taking the Arba Minim that can have a major impact on us. The Torah, by placing *hadar* at this place of prominence, has already made a powerful statement about the nature of our work. Just the awareness of all our mitzvos as being contained within the overarching theme of attaining *hadar* affects the way we look at mitzvos throughout the year. It empowers us to seek the beauty in each mitzvah, as well as how it beautifies us ourselves. Our practice of *hiddur mitzvah* should be a reflection of the spiritual beauty attained through the mitzvos, and it should be geared toward attaining a general spiritual beauty through the cumulative effects of all of the mitzvos expressed through the *hadar* of the Arba Minim.

The mitzvah of the Arba Minim echoes the concept of *hiddur mitzvah*, but possibly even more powerfully. This particular mitzvah, in practice and understanding, brings us back to our initial encounter with the beauty and splendor of God Himself. It signifies the culmination of, and, by extension, places all of our strivings within the context of, our lifelong mission of "beautifying ourselves before God," thereby reflecting and refracting something of God's beauty and splendor.

Vivacity Reclaimed

CHAPTER 13

"It's Alive!" Revisited

In the first part of this book we focused on the joy evoked by the Arba Minim. One factor that contributes toward their ability to elicit joy, we argued, is their vitality. This is true of all of the Minim in a general sense, and we argued that it plays a central role in the type of joy evoked by the Aravah.

Is it possible, though, that the aliveness of the species is more central than simply serving as catalyst for joy? What if it is has inherent significance? What if, indeed, their aliveness is central to the essence of the mitzvah of the Arba Minim?

The *Moreh Nevuchim* notes that the Arba Minim are unique in their ability to maintain life and moisture for a period of time.[1] He understands that this is important for pragmatic reasons: practically, it is easier to obtain fresh specimens of the Arba Minim throughout Sukkos than of other species.

Rabbeinu Bachya,[2] however, noting the same property of each of the Arba Minim, attributes inherent significance to this property of vivacity. Moreover, he notes that a dry Lulav is disqualified, and according to the *Talmud Yerushalmi*,[3] this is derived from the verse in *Tehillim*, "The dead cannot praise God."[4] It is clear that vivacity is a significant

---

1   3:43.
2   Commentary on the Torah, s.v. *v'al derech ha'seichel.*
3   *Sukkah* 3:1.
4   *Tehillim* 115:17.

component of this mitzvah, and, moreover, that Chazal see the mitzvah of Lulav as one of utilizing "aliveness" itself to express praise of God.

Triad of Vivacity

These clues lead Rabbeinu Bachya to posit that the theme of the mitzvah is indeed that of life, aliveness, vivacity. He points out that the Creator, the Torah, and Klal Yisrael are all described as being "alive."[5] Hashem, of course, is referred to as "the living God." The Torah, Divine gift from God, is called the "Path of Life," "Torah of Life," and so forth. And the Jewish People, recipients of the Torah, are referred to as the "living nation," as the Torah states, "You who cling to God...you are all alive today."[6]

Rabbeinu Bachya explains that we take the Minim as a symbol of *darkei ha'chaim*, the paths that lead to life, and as a tool with which to praise the living God.

Rabbeinu Bachya's comment opens up new worlds of understanding both at the macro-level of understanding what Torah is all about, as well as at the micro-level of understanding the mitzvah of the Arba Minim.

At the macro-level, Rabbeinu Bachya has identified the centrality of *chaim*, a quality which defines God, Torah, and the Jewish People. This forces us to rethink our relationship with and understanding of each of the members of this triad.

At the micro-level, he has then tied that quality of life to simple plant life and has brought our attention to the fact that the mitzvah of the Arba Minim is in fact designed to make that connection.

All of these ideas need to be explored and investigated.

Chaim—Basic Definitions

Why, we might ask, is the "aliveness" of God, Torah, and the Jewish People, respectively, so central?

Before exploring the meaning and centrality of the "aliveness" of God, Torah, and the Jewish People, we need to revisit the concept of "life"

---

5   See also *Avos D'Rabi Nosson* (34:10), which lists ten entities that are called "alive." The first
      three members of the list are Hashem, Torah, and the Jewish People.

6   *Devarim* 4:4.

itself.[7] We can begin with the Hebrew word *chaim*. Until now we have translated it as "life;" but that word does not really capture the essence of what it means.

In fact, it is difficult to find a word that does justice to this concept. Vitality, Vivacity, Animation, Liveliness, Verve, Sparkle, Exuberance, Zest, Buoyancy, Effervescence, Enthusiasm, Energy, Vigor, Dynamism, Spirit, Fire, Zing, Vital spark, Life force, Elan vital, Vibrancy, Liveness, Transcendence—all of these are given by the thesaurus as synonyms of "life." But—none of these words really capture the meaning of *chaim*. In reality, *chaim* includes all of the above and infinitely more.

In fact, it is only to be expected that there be no word—nor a combination of words—in our vernacular to adequately capture the meaning of the word *"chaim."* Keep in mind that this is a word that is used both to describe the "life" of a fly or even a shoot of grass, on the one hand, and the transcendent, ineffable, infinite existence of *"Elokim chaim,"* the living God. It refers to both a state of physiological being of the cellular organism in our physical world, yet at the same time to the eternal, qualitatively different state of being of man's spiritual essence in the Eternal world. *Chaim* is an idea that cannot be translated; the best we can do is use other words and metaphors to glimpse an inkling of its true meaning.

Contemplating Aliveness

Before investigating the centrality of the aliveness of the Creator, Torah, and the Jewish People, however, we would do well to ponder the very concept of life itself. What is it? What does it mean to be alive? On the one hand, life is the simplest of concepts. It is, after all, the basis of everything we think, feel, experience, and say; without life there would be none of that. I live; therefore, I think, feel, speak, etc.

---

7   For a comprehensive discussion of the concepts of the vivacity of God, Torah, and Yisrael, as well as the very concept of life itself, see Rav Shlomo Wolbe's *Daas Shlomo: Maamarei Yemei HaRatzon*, pp. 293–340, as well as the treatise on *chaim* that serves as the closing section of the second volume of Rav Wolbe's *Alei Shur*. Interestingly, although Rav Wolbe does not cite *Rabbeinu Bachya*, he explores the "aliveness" of God, Torah, and the Jewish people, as well as the very concept of life itself. Some of the thoughts that follow are based on Rav Wolbe's comprehensive treatment of the topic.

The Mystery of Life

Despite its ubiquity, however, life is perhaps the most elusive concept we encounter. The Chazon Ish, reflecting on the mystery of life, does not mince words in expressing our complete inability to apprehend its essence: "We know that it exists, but we do not know what it is. We use all sorts of fancy terms to describe it—*nefesh, neshamah, ruach*—but these terms cannot change the fact that we are clueless as to the essence of life."[8]

It is said that Moshe was privy to forty-nine of the fifty "gates of wisdom" in this universe. Rav Shlomo Wolbe[9] cites the Gaon of Vilna who explains that the fiftieth gate of wisdom, which Moshe was unable to attain, refers to the nature of "life." Put differently, the secret of life is the secret of the universe.

Why do people, especially children, have an obsession with animals? There is an entire industry of zoos to which millions of people the world over flock. If you've ever seen children riding in a car passing cows or horses, you may have seen their incredible excitement. What is so exciting about a cow munching hay?

The sight of any living thing should be shocking to us. If it is not, it is only because we are so used to the commodity of life that we have become inured to it. It is only when we see a life form to which we are not consistently exposed that we intuitively appreciate the great miracle of life.

Is there something more amazing about elephants than about human beings? Are giraffes inherently more exotic than people? If anything, the opposite is true. Human beings are infinitely more complex than any other living thing. In fact, were animals to have the capacity for wonder, it is probable that they would be propelled to great spiritual heights simply by seeing a human being. It would seem, rather, that encountering a life form that we are not used to seeing frees us from our ennui and allows us to take note of that amazing quality—life itself.

---

8   *Emunah U'Bitachon* 1:2.

9   *Daas Shlomo.*

In the words of the Chazon Ish:[10]

> *Abundance of habituation dulls the natural sense of amazement we should feel at the sight of any life form, simply at its being a form of life. [Conversely,] we do experience a sense of wonder when we see specific life forms which are not as common, or at seeing unusual looking creatures [since we are not habituated to seeing them].*

Our excitement at seeing an exotic and unusual creature should teach us about our potential for amazement at apprehending any life form.

It is, of course, the existence of life itself which stymies scientists who believe they could explain the development of all life-forms based on evolution. The problem is, evolution is possible only once one living cell already exists. Alas, no one has the foggiest notion of how the first living cell developed.

A corollary of life is consciousness. Plant life is also alive, but full-fledged life involves another dimension, that of consciousness, which exists only in sentient beings. Consciousness is another bane to evolutionists, many of whom recognize that evolution cannot explain this dimension.

We may not be able to apprehend the essence of life, but we experience it in ourselves and all around us. Perhaps the recognition and awareness that we cannot grasp the essence of life—that life is simply ineffable—is itself the best tool for apprehending and appreciating it.

Spark of the Divine

That the essence of life is so difficult to comprehend should not surprise us.

All life, writes Rav Shlomo Wolbe—even the life force of the lowliest worm, indeed even the simplest life-form—is a spark of Divine life.[11] Though, of course, everything emanates from God, it is life, which, as

---

10   *Emunah U'Bitachon* 1:7.
11   *Daas Shlomo*, p. 298.

the *Mesilas Yesharim* writes,[12] "is that which is most closely affiliated with God." Any and every form of life is a direct pipeline to God who is known as *Elokim chaim*, not only because all life stems from Him, but because that term best describes His essence to the degree that we can comprehend it. Is it any wonder, then, that we cannot grasp the essence of even the most infinitesimal, simple spark of life?

If, however, God is epitomized by life, and any life form is a spark of that life, then it is through apprehending life that we can somehow apprehend God. By developing our awareness and appreciation of the existence of life—whether in ourselves, other people, or other forms of existence—we give ourselves the tools to apprehend something about God, the ultimate form of life.

Nefesh HaTzomachas—Plant Life

As human beings we are not only alive but conscious and sentient as well. Nevertheless, it is the form of life we call "life," which exists even with plant life, that is the basis of our consciousness. Consciousness is an enhanced life form but is based on the basic life force that exists as plant life. In Rabbinic language this is known as the *nefesh ha'tzomachas*.[13]

Our project of apprehending human life must begin with the development of an appreciation of the miracle of plant life. In fact, the secret to all life is contained in the *nefesh ha'tzomachas*, with all other forms of life being simply a development and expansion of the basic life force contained in plant life. (Perhaps it is not a coincidence that it was the "tree of life" that contained the secret of immortality.)

The *Malbim* offers the important insight that among all living things, the commodity of life itself is most clearly ostensive in plant life.[14] Only plant life must remain connected to the ground in order to remain alive. And only plant life regenerates itself when part of it is cut. The higher a life form goes, the more subtle, the more spiritual it becomes, and the less obvious and ostensive its life force becomes. Once consciousness

---

12   Chap. 26.
13   See, for example, the Vilna Gaon's *Aderes Eliyahu* to *Bereishis* 1:26.
14   *Bereishis* 1:25.

and sentience are added, those qualities can overwhelm the simple life force and subsume it, or at least deflect our attention from it.

For these reasons, if we wish to sensitize ourselves to the mystery of life itself, we must look to the simplicity of plant life. We will return to this idea later.

CHAPTER 14

Triad of Life

Having contemplated the very existence of life, we are poised to return to Rabbeinu Bachya's triad of Hashem, Torah and Israel. The observation that all of these are "alive," obviously does not refer only to the fact that they are alive and not dead. It means that all of these possess levels of "aliveness" not found in any other being or entity. It means that they are truly alive in the fullest sense of the word. Let us survey how vivacity is a trademark feature of each of the three members of the triad.

The Living God

Hashem is referred to as "the living God" only once in the Torah. However, the Neviim use the term numerous times. And it is mentioned numerous times by David HaMelech in *Tehillim*.

Many Greek philosophers believed in an infinite being that is the source of all existence. However, that "being" in their minds is aloof, and there is no dynamic interaction with it. In fact, many believed that there was no act of creation; they thought the world had always existed, albeit as an extension or shadow of the unmoved mover. This being is a "real" one, but not a "living" one!

The Giver of the Torah, by contrast, is described by the Torah in such vivid and dynamic terms that it becomes necessary for our great commentaries to remind us not to take these descriptions too literally. It is abundantly clear from the entirety of the Torah that God conjured the universe into existence as a willful, conscious, and dynamic act of creativity; and that He continues to interact consciously, willfully, and dynamically with His world, and particularly with the Jewish People.

Aside from describing God Himself, as it were, as the living God, *Sefer Daniel* refers to Hashem as "the life-giver of the world."[1] This appellation is incorporated into our liturgy in numerous places: We begin and complete *Pesukei D'Zimrah* daily with it. Toward the end of *Baruch She'amar* we address God as: "Unique One; life-giver of the worlds," and the very end of *Yishtabach* culminates with the words: "King, God, life-giver of the worlds."

Though we are reminded again and again that we know nothing about the essence of God, the Torah itself conveys to us God's "aliveness" and "dynamism," as it were. And our primary modality of relating to God is in the capacity of "life-giver of the worlds."

Not only is God Himself a God of life, and the life-giver of the universe, but His "word," that is, the words pertaining to the future that He conveyed to his Neviim, are also "alive." Not only will they come true, they are most certainly alive; God's words continue to silently, but vibrantly and dynamically, do the job of laying the groundwork for their ultimate fruition.

Apprehending Life

How can we connect, in our own minds, with the vivacity of God? We can only begin with our own apprehension of life, beginning with, perhaps, ourselves, and continuing with other primitive or sophisticated forms of life by which we are surrounded. We can then contemplate the fact that all life emanates from "the life-giver of the universe." Certainly, the source of all this vibrancy is no less vibrant than the derivatives. As the Psalmist asks rhetorically, "He who affixed the ear, can He not hear? He that formed the eye, can He not see?"[2] To which we might add: He who is the source of all life and vibrancy—is He not fully alive?

---

1   *Daniel* 12:7.
2   *Tehillim* 94:9.

The greater our awareness of and sensitivity to the mysterious nature of life, and thus the greater our sense of the reality and vibrancy of life, the greater our ability to project from that life back onto its Author.

Beyond being the source of all life as we know it, God Himself is synonymous with life itself. *Elokim chaim* means not only that God is alive but that He is the epitome of life itself.[3]

As the *Mesilas Yesharim* explains, the commodity that is most intimately associated with Hashem is that of life.[4] For that reason, the highest rung on the ladder of spiritual ascent is that of resurrecting the dead. When a person reaches a sufficient degree of closeness to Hashem, he is able to draw life itself from Hashem. This, explains the *Mesilas Yesharim*, is how the Neviim were able to revivify the dead.

We might be accustomed to thinking of Hashem in more religious terms, but at a deeper level we need to understand and internalize that God is first and foremost life itself, that He is the source of our own aliveness, and that He wishes for us to become more and more alive. In the words recited in the *Yamim Nora'im* liturgy, Hashem is the "King Who desires life."

Ironically, instead of noticing the incredible life force coursing through this world and then working backward to perceive the source of this life, we can sometimes allow the opposite to happen. An incorrect and stultified perception of who and what God is can strangulate our perception of life coursing through the world. Therefore, a prerequisite to understanding anything about Hashem is internalizing the reality that He is truly the "God of life" as well as the "living God."

Rav Hirsch notes that it is clear throughout the Torah and *Neviim* that it was customary for idolaters to worship specifically under fresh trees.[5] Why so? Rav Hirsch explains that they were so dazzled by expressions of life that they were unable to see past it, relating to this life force as a god on its own. Truly relating to God, then, is the opposite of this: taking note of the life force flowing through the world and working

---

3   *Maharal*, Introduction to *Derech Chaim*.
4   Chap. 26.
5   *Devarim* 12:2.

backward to grasping that there is one source, infinitely more alive, to all of this life.[6]

אלקים חיים! זוהי בשורת התורה כולה, על כל מצוותיה!

The living God! This is the revelation of the entirety of Torah, with all of its mitzvos!

Alei Shur II, p. 744

God of Life

A prerequisite to conceptualizing Hashem as the God of life is the recognition that He wills life for us. As we affirm in the special sections added to our prayers during the Ten Days of *teshuvah*, Hashem is "the King Who desires life;" yet we may not always sense this. The world teems with life, but at the same time, there is no lack of death, suffering, and ostensible uselessness all around us.

Affirmation of Hashem as the God Who desires life calls for a certain degree of *emunah* (faith). What is this faith based on? What gives us the strength to persevere and relate to the living God as such?

The Gemara sees the word "faith" as corresponding to the order of *Zeraim*, which deals with plant life.[7] *Tosafos* citing the *Yerushalmi* explains that this is because for one to plant, it is necessary to have faith in God.[8] Every endeavor, including planting seeds, is fraught with uncertainty and doubt. Will it succeed? Is it worth continuing on? It is only faith that makes it possible to hope for success, for the emergence of life.

---

6   Rav S.R. Hirsch translates *"raanan"* as a tree that remains green year-round, thus serving as a powerful expression of life, which attracted the idolaters. It is interesting that the mitzvah of the Arba Minim is the direct inversion of this tendency—we take these plants which, as noted by Rabbeinu Bachya, retain their greenness and life, and use them to praise the One God.

7   *Shabbos* 31a.

8   Ad loc., s.v. *emunas*.

The Sages refer to God with a number of terms, depending on the context. What is interesting, though, is the term the Sages use for God in this context. Some examples are the Holy One, blessed be He and Master of the Universe. In this particular context, the Sages use the term "the Life-Giver of the Universe" to refer to God. What is the significance of this particular way of referring to Hashem?

The faith evinced by the planter in his act of planting is not a generic faith in God. It is faith specifically in the capacity of "Life-Giver of the Universe." What gives the planter this faith to begin with is the very existence of life itself, which can obviously be traced back to a source. The planter observes life, believes in it, sees it emanating from a source, and taps into that source with his act of planting.

That Chazal see this model as a paradigm of *emunah* is illuminating. It means that the key to developing true faith—a true awareness of God and His presence in this world—is that of becoming receptive to, and aware of, the force of life itself, and furthermore, believing in that force as a reality that can then be traced back to the Life-Giver.[9]

Torah of Life

The Torah is referred to as *orach chaim*, the path of life, as well as the tree of life. In our daily liturgy we ask Hashem to teach us *chukei chaim*, life-giving laws. In the Ashkenazic version of *Shemoneh Esreh*, we acknowledge that God has, with the "light of His countenance," bequeathed to us *Toras Chaim*, a Torah of life.

The Torah is a Torah of life first and foremost because it is the word of the living God. But there is another, perhaps deeper meaning of the term "living Torah." All wisdom emanates from God, but there is something unique about Torah. Torah is not just a body of information or knowledge. It is alive and dynamic, with a reality and a life of its own. Part of this is perhaps its ability to adapt itself to any situation and

---

9 In *Bamidbar Rabbah* 13:16, an even stronger term is used: "He believes in the life of the Universe and plants." In this formulation, as explained by the commentators, we refer to God not simply as the "Life-Giver" but of the "Life Force" itself, which is ever present in all parts of the universe.

to find new solutions for new situations that crop up over the course of history.

Torah is called a Torah of life because through it we achieve robust and authentic living in both this world and the eternal one. This is made possible both because the content is one which points us and educates us toward true life, as well as the fact that the Torah affords us a connection to the living God Himself. More immediately, Torah provides the framework and ability to be truly alive in this world. We are fully alive when we are able to utilize every moment and every situation for truly meaningful and lasting achievement. It is not only satisfaction that we feel at doing this but a real sense of aliveness.

A deeper meaning of *Toras Chaim* is that Torah is specially designed to become completely enmeshed with every facet of our lives. Rather than remaining a guidebook that tells us from the outside how to live our lives, the Torah, a living entity itself, emanating as it does from the source of all life, becomes implanted into the human organism and becomes an integral part of it. It is planted within the living soul of the human being and grows and sprouts naturally along with it.

It is not for naught that concerning the Torah we are taught, "Each day it should be as if it is new."[10]

If all the above is true of Torah life and observance, it is most certainly true of Torah study. Studying Torah, when done properly, is truly life-giving, and those people who invest in it wholeheartedly come to regard it as life itself.

Underlying Life Force

Is Torah complex or simple? Is life complex or simple? On the one hand, there is nothing more complex than a living organism! But that complexity is not the life force itself; rather, it is the infrastructure through which life expresses itself. Life itself is an exceedingly simple commodity.

The same is true of the Torah. It is exceedingly complex, deep, and broad. All the characteristics the Torah wishes to instill in us are

---

10   See *Rashi, Shemos* 19:1.

manifestations of true life. Yet the inner life force running through it is simple.[11]

> "These are the mitzvos, the laws, and the statutes which a human being shall do and live through them!"
>
> *Vayikra 18:5*
>
> "The sum total of the qualities acquired via performing the mitzvos of the Torah is—life!"
>
> *Rav Shamshon Raphael Hirsch, Commentary to Chumash*

The Living Nation

The Jewish People, as noted by Rabbeinu Bachya, are referred to as "alive" through their connection to the living God: "And you, who cleave to Hashem, your God, are all alive today."[12] Inasmuch as God is the God of life, the Jewish People, whose very existence revolves around its connection to God, is truly the nation of life. And the Torah of life lives itself out solely through the nation of Israel.

Yaakov Avinu, after whom Klal Yisrael is named, never died. So powerful was his connection to life that it could not be broken.[13] The Jewish People, collectively, have remained alive over millennia—which defies the laws of nature. And the Jewish spark of life is what has caused individuals who are very, very far away to remain alive in their search for truth and meaning.

The Land of the Living

It is well known that Eretz Yisrael—called "the land of life"[14]—lay desolate, dead, for thousands of years when its children were in *galus* (exile).

---

11   See *Devarim Rabbah* 11:6: "The entire Torah, and all wisdom, is one simple thing."
12   *Devarim* 4:4.
13   *Taanis* 5b. See also *Gur Aryeh, Bereishis* 49:13.
14   *Tehillim* 116:9 (see *Rashi* there).

Suddenly, when the Jewish People—the people of life—returned, the land became alive and sprung into full bloom.

Fully Alive

We are truly alive by virtue of our connection to the living God through His living Torah. However, the converse is also true: to the degree that we are truly alive, we are able to apprehend and connect to the aliveness of our Creator. The Gemara states that while the righteous are alive even after death, the wicked are considered dead even while physically alive. The Midrash elaborates on this:[15]

> *The wicked person is considered dead because he sees the sun rise and fails to recite the blessing of Yotzer Ohr; he sees the sun set and fails to recite the blessing of Maariv Aravim; he eats and drinks but does not bless Hashem. The righteous, on the other hand, are considered alive because they bless the Creator for everything that they eat and drink, and for everything that they hear. And not only during their lives; even after they die, they continue to bless and thank Hashem.[16]*

Clearly, part of the unique aliveness conferred upon members of the Jewish People is the sensitivity to every detail and nuance in our world, and the ability to connect to the source of it all.

Broadening Our Scope

Above, we pondered the centrality of life in Torah, but in fact it actually goes deeper than that. We need to take a step back and look at the whole picture.

Man was created to be immortal. His very creation was accomplished when God "blew into his nostrils a breath of life," which, the commentaries tell us, was a breath of God's own "life" itself. That is, he was above death. When he sins and becomes mortal, it's not just a question

---

15   *Tanchuma*, end of *V'zos Haberachah*.

16   Perhaps this is a reference to the message conveyed by the *Tosefta* (*Berachos* 6:27, as understood by *Rashi* to *Berachos* 63a): "Practice praising the Creator in this world, so that you will continue praising Him eternally in the next world!"

of how long I will live. Becoming mortal means that every moment has lost its connection with true aliveness.

Adam is told that "On the day you eat from this tree you will die."[17] This did not only mean that he would become mortal and eventually die. It means that he would lose his true aliveness—immediately. His ultimate demise would simply be an indication that his life ceased to be true life, which in fact never comes to an end. Not only would he not be truly alive, but the entire trajectory of his life would be one headed toward death.

The entire story of humanity begins after man becomes mortal by sinning, and the rest of the story is man's quest to transcend death and regain immortality i.e., life. The entirety of Torah and mitzvos is about transcending death; this, at a deeper level, is the meaning of the verse stating, "These are the laws…that a man shall do and live through them."

The event of receiving the Torah directly from Hashem was supposed to be a moment at which the Jewish People would transcend death.[18] Again, sin interfered, and we are plunged back into a world in which death is ubiquitous, back on the long-term trajectory toward immortality.

Throughout *Tanach*, exile is depicted as death.[19] The *Kuzari*,[20] *Ramban*,[21] and the *Vilna Gaon*,[22] describe the state of the Jewish People ever since the destruction of the Beis Hamikdash as "dead." The redemption will be a revivification of the Jewish People as a whole.

What we are ultimately aiming for is the time when death will be abolished. Not only will we live forever, but the very concept of death and destruction, of less than the most complete and most full existence, will cease.

At the center of the Garden of Eden stood the Tree of Life. The staff utilized by Moshe to execute the miracles that took place at the Exodus

---

17   *Bereishis* 2:17.
18   *Shabbos* 147a.
19   See, for example, *Yechezkel* 37; *Hoshea* 6:2; *Chavakuk* 3:2.
20   3:11.
21   *Bereishis* 47:28.
22   *Likutim*, printed at the end of the *Sifra D'Tzniusa*.

from Egypt was taken from the Tree of Life. That staff, continues the Midrash, will be passed on to the Mashiach, and it is that staff, part and parcel of the Tree of Life, that will be utilized by Mashiach to usher in the era in which true life will be realized.[23]

In Rav Pinchas ben Yair's model of spiritual growth,[24] which serves as the basis of the *Mesilas Yesharim*, a person ascends the levels of Divine service, culminating in *techiyas ha'meisim*, the Revivification of the Dead. This is a direct parallel to the trajectory of the world, which must ultimately reach transcendence of death.

The story of our lives, individually, collectively, and historically, is the quest for true life.

---

23 See *Pirkei D'Rabi Eliezer*, chap. 40, with commentary of *Radal*, n. 7 and 17.
24 *Avodah Zarah* 20b.

CHAPTER 15

Return to Life

Sukkos and Celebrating Life

Before returning to Rabbeinu Bachya's vision of the Arba Minim as symbolic of the aliveness of the triad of God, Torah, and Israel, let us examine the backdrop of this activity: the festival of Sukkos. Why is Sukkos the appropriate time for this?

Sukkos is the climax of the year with all its material and spiritual strivings, the goal of all of which is...life. It is the *Chag Ha'Asif*, the festival of gathering, and the physical gathering of the year's produce is symbolic of our gathering together the fruits of our spiritual efforts from the past year. As the third and final of the three *Regalim*, which represents the full cycle of the Jewish People's maturation, Sukkos is the time when we celebrate the fullness of our relationship with the living God.

Sukkos also comes on the heels of the *Yamim Nora'im*. On Rosh Hashanah and Yom Kippur we seek life. During the Aseres Yemei Teshuvah, beginning on Rosh Hashanah and continuing through Yom Kippur, we consistently and repeatedly beg God to remember us for life, to write us in the book of life, and so on. On Rosh Hashanah and Yom Kippur we reach a certain new level in our connection to the source of life, our appreciation for what constitutes real life, and that expresses itself on Sukkos with the Arba Minim.

The Living Minim

Let us now return to the mitzvah of the Arba Minim itself. Rabbeinu Bachya, pointing out the salience of life in this mitzvah, had explained that the Arba Minim are to symbolize "the pathways of life." What does this mean, and what is the significance of this?

At the simplest level, this idea is eminently understandable. We use the Minim to rejoice before God, primarily over our great fortune in our association with Him and the opportunity to serve Him. For someone who truly appreciates the nature of God, Torah, and Israel, it is only natural that we celebrate our association with the source of life and with His life-giving Torah, as well as our own status as the living nation, with tangible, physical expression of life and vivacity. Doing so not only expresses our joy over our attachment to true life but also serves to cement that perception.

Perhaps, though, there is another level to this idea, one which is more relevant to many of us today as well as more transformational.

It might be suggested that the mitzvah of affirming life with the Arba Minim has two faces. Under ideal circumstances, for individuals who have indeed reached a full and robust recognition of the aliveness of God, Torah, and Israel, this mitzvah would simply allow this awareness to bubble over and express itself.

The problem, though, is that while we might all nod and agree to the descriptions of "the living God," "a Torah of life," and "the living nation," this is not necessarily our inner perception. It is all too easy to lapse into perceptions that do not necessarily associate Torah, Hashem, or Klal Yisrael, with life or aliveness. Perhaps we have learned to think of God in other terms. We may have come to view Torah and mitzvos as a burden that impinge on our sense of aliveness, instead of as the source of life. Paradoxically, the Torah of life, or parts of it, might have become anything but that for us. If the Torah describes its mitzvos as those by which, and through which, "man shall live," we might secretly, or at least subconsciously, feel as if God has given us "laws with which we cannot live."[1]

---

1   *Yechezkel* 20:25.

Our perception of the Jewish People, as well, may have become jaded, so that we no longer see ourselves and others as members of the living nation. One might wonder whether the aspect of the mitzvah dealing with life and vivacity is relevant to someone who finds himself in this situation.

This, perhaps, is the second face of the mitzvah of the Arba Minim. The mitzvah serves not only as a smooth expression of the truths it represents, but also as a reminder of sorts, as a reconfiguration of our identity and recalibration of our mission.

The mitzvah of the Arba Minim reminds us of the true nature of Torah, our relationship with Hashem, and our essence as the Jewish People: aliveness. It reminds us to seek out the essential life contained within each and every mitzvah. For seven days, we recalibrate our relationship with Hashem, with His mitzvos and Torah life, and with the Jewish People, bringing it back into the context of life and vibrancy.

We know that the ultimate reward is that of the next world, which is referred to as "the life of *Olam Haba*." For many of us, talk of life in the next world is abstract and extremely difficult to relate to. It becomes necessary to remind ourselves that what we are ultimately striving for is life. It is, of course, life of an entirely different order of magnitude; but it is life, nonetheless. Engaging the Arba Minim with an understanding that they represent the Torah, the path to true life, reminds us of this reality.

If we have strayed, over the course of the year, from a pristine recognition of the true nature of God, Torah, and mitzvos, and the life we are to achieve through Torah, the Arba Minim bring us back. They remind us to approach every mitzvah like planting a shoot; each encounter with God as an experience of tapping into the ultimate force of life. If we have begun performing mitzvos by rote, or studying Torah in such a manner that we do not derive life-giving spiritual sustenance from it, the species urge us to recalibrate; to find the mode of Torah study that can nourish our souls, and to design our mitzvah observance in such a way that we feel the life-giving nature of the mitzvos.

The Little Things

Of course, the idea that waving around some botanical samples can teach our subconscious minds that Torah is all about true life, might seem preposterous. Furthermore, it would appear that there is little or no connection between primitive plant life and the transcendent, spiritual life that we speak of when we talk about Hashem and His Torah.

Is it not absurd to believe that handling some botanical specimens will somehow enhance our ability to connect to the unique vitality to be had only in the presence of the living God? And does the linking of profound spiritual truths to some leaves, twigs, and fruit not trivialize those truths?

Indeed, it is profoundly absurd. It is also profoundly true, though, because the human condition itself is profoundly absurd, too. It is a fact of life that no matter how lofty and compelling an idea, no matter how spiritually energizing a given concept, until we experience it on a primal, visceral level, it remains abstract and aloof.

We can talk all day long about life, aliveness, and the fact that all of the above are to be found in Torah and in Torah alone. But talk is talk. It goes with the wind and remains abstract. And we remain skeptical. What will make us realize that this is real? What will drive this reality home to the deepest recesses of our consciousness?

In an impossibly absurd, yet profoundly true, insight into the human organism, the Torah understands that the lofty spiritual truths about the living God, the living Torah, and the living nation, become real within the organism known as a human being only when anchored to an actual lived experience involving the most basic life form.

Does linking these truths with botanical samples trivialize them? To the contrary: it is only through linking them with each other that these spiritual truths move from the realm of abstract platitudes to lived reality. Far from trivializing them, association of the aliveness of God, Torah, and Yisrael, with a real-life experience of simple life force, is what makes these ideas come alive. The life force abiding within the specimen arouses the life force within the human being. Within the context of serving Hashem, this turns our intellectual recognition of the life-giving qualities of Torah and our relationship with God into a living, breathing reality.

If we in fact see no connection between simple plant life and the aliveness of God, Torah, and Israel, perhaps that is exactly what this mitzvah is all about. To the extent that we insist that although Torah is all about life, it is nevertheless a different type of aliveness, a spiritual form of life, which in fact has nothing in common with the simple, biological plant or animal life; the mitzvah of the Arba Minim corrects that perception.

The Life Continuum

As we have tried to explain above, life is life; there is a vast continuum in terms of lower and higher forms of life, but there is no inherent difference between the life force flowing through a branch or a leaf and the eternal, transcendent life to which we aspire. Someone who truly senses Torah as alive, who truly relates to Hashem as the living God, would undoubtedly automatically associate any living thing with God and Torah life.

Divorcing the aliveness of God and Torah from the simple, unvarnished life force we encounter all around us effectively sterilizes it. It pulls the rug out from under any true recognition of their "live" nature. For after all is said and done, as living biological entities we can only relate to life through its lowest level. But when we do relate to it at that level, and then understand how all forms of life, including spiritual life, are part of one continuum, we are then able to relate to spirituality and Torah as true life.

It is only when we grasp the meaning of the commodity called life, at its lowest form, that we begin to understand what it means when we say that Hashem and Torah are "alive." Life is life. There is fuller or less full life, but all life emanates from the same life force.

Looking at Torah through the lens of simple plant life reminds us that what the Torah wants for us is not something outside of and above our simple, uncomplicated sense of aliveness and yearning for life. At its deepest level, the Torah speaks to our simple, primal life force and seeks to elevate, enrich, and actualize it.

This is true of the entirety of Torah, but it is easy to lose sight of it. The mitzvah of the Lulav, by engaging that primal, primitive life force directly brings us back to the proper perspective.

Plant Life

Plant life is actually the ideal thing to capture the spark of life itself. As noted earlier, all other forms of life are simply enhanced, more sophisticated iterations of the same life force. But the enhancements and sophistication can cause us to lose sight of the life force itself. It is only when we encounter an embodiment of simple, uncomplicated aliveness, without even the added property of consciousness, that we are able to take full notice of the life coursing through it.

We harness this simple but infinitely powerful spark of life and incorporate it into our Divine service. In doing so we bring the totality of our *avodas Hashem* into the realm of life and aliveness.

Although life seems like one simple concept, the more we examine it and see what flows from it and what is included in it, the more we come to realize how rich and all-inclusive it is.

In celebrating and experiencing our full and robust aliveness, we need something tangible that can bring us to the simplest, most overt "life force." We need to engage the most primitive level of life, that of *nefesh ha'tzomachas*, within the context of Divine service and rejoicing, in order to be able to fully experience our relationship with God and Torah as a fully alive one.

The Torah commands us to utilize the *nefesh ha'tzomachas* to contextualize our *avodas Hashem*. We are to engage it, to become absorbed in it to the point that it defines our consciousness while we celebrate before God. This in turn transfers the aliveness that we feel upon encountering plant life into our relationship with all that is Godly; and it places our relationship with that which is Godly within the context of life and vitality. *Nefesh ha'tzomachas* brings us to the point of life itself at its simplest, most basic, and purest, and allows to recast our relationship with Hashem and mitzvos in this spirit.

Like life itself, Torah is externally complex but internally simple. The mitzvah of the Arba Minim allows us to bring the complexity of Torah back to its underlying simplicity.

We might have thought it more effective to have a seven-day, intensive seminar about aliveness of God and Torah, with workshops delivered and facilitated by world renowned speakers and educators. Surely, we would imagine, this would be more powerful than simply waving some branches and a fruit! The Torah understands that this would not do the trick. As living beings, we can only connect to the concept of aliveness via an actual encounter with a manifestly and vividly alive thing. Yes, we might know and study all about the aliveness and vivacity of Rabbeinu Bachya's triad, but without spending time with the simple Lulav, we will not manage to convince our own psyche of those truths.

Aliveness Experienced

Life, we suggested, cannot be defined in words or grasped by the mind. It can only be experienced. This experience is had through encountering the Arba Minim in all their primitive life. The Arba Minim become the centerpiece for a week, with all our attention focused on it, to the point that we immerse ourselves in the concept of actual physical aliveness. It creates an entire world suffused with vibrancy and vivacity within which we function. Our intellectual and theoretical understanding of the aliveness of God, Torah, and Israel becomes suffused with our experience of, and immersion in, the most basic of life-forms and the life force flowing through it.[2]

It is crucial to note that it is not simply the exposure to plant life that has this effect on us. Surely, we could do this even without it being a mitzvah—but it would not have the same impact. It is specifically the knowledge that we stand commanded by God Himself to do this that makes the impression on the psyche. It is the awareness that God Himself, in His infinite knowledge and understanding of human nature, has deemed it necessary and crucial for us to engage in this act as a way

---

2   Of course, a prerequisite to this is the openness to being affected by the sight and presence of plant life. If the Torah instructs us to use plant life to arouse within us associations between Torah and aliveness, surely it is presupposing that we are deeply affected by plant life.

of celebrating our relationship with Him and His Torah. This, fused with the actual action of taking the species, has a powerful effect on us.

In fact, as we mentioned in an earlier discussion, the mitzvah guides us and teaches us just by its very existence, even before we perform it. Just the knowledge that the Torah wishes us to engage in this activity already creates an opening of understanding about how Torah perceives itself. This is certainly true if the Torah places this at the pinnacle of the spiritual year, sending us a powerful message about what it is all about.

שח רבינו בתחילת חודש ניסן ואמר: בחורף כל העשבים וכל הצמחים כולם מתים...וכשבא הקיץ, כולם נתעוררים וחיים. ואז טוב ויפה מאד כשיוצאים לשוח בשדה 'שיחה זו תפילה' ותחינה ותשוקה וגעגועים להשם יתברך.

Rav Nachman of Breslov said, at the beginning of the month of Nissan: In the winter, all of the grass and the plants die...When spring comes, they awaken to life. At that time, it is good to go out to the fields to speak to Hashem and to feel desire for closeness to Him.

Sichos HaRan 98

Let us examine some additional properties of life which are brought home to us through our involvement with the Minim.

Growth

A property of life is growth and sprouting. Life is never static. Plant life is always growing, and animal life is constantly replenishing itself.

Humankind, specifically, is called "*adam*" because the first human being was taken from the ground. But were not animals taken from the ground, and do not trees and plants issue from the ground?

The *Maharal* explains that the earth is unique in that it is pure potential.[3] Its potential becomes reality through that which springs forth growth from it: trees, fruits, and plant life. This is exactly the concept

---

3   *Tiferes Yisrael*, chap. 3.

of a human being, who starts out as pure potential and then comes to fruition through achieving perfection. For this reason, explains the *Maharal*, human perfection and achievement is referred to in *Tanach* as fruit, as it is written, "Tell the righteous all is good; for they will enjoy the fruits of their actions."[4] Man's potential for dynamic growth defines his very essence.[5]

The realization that Torah is all about life puts us into a growth mindset. We become aware that living a Torah life means planting ourselves and allowing ourselves to sprout.[6]

> וְהָיָה כְּעֵץ שָׁתוּל עַל פַּלְגֵי מָיִם...וְעָלֵהוּ לֹא יִבּוֹל...
>
> [The righteous person] is like a tree planted firmly on streams of water...whose leaves do not wither...
>
> *Tehillim 1:3*

Naturalness

Beyond growth, life means naturalness. There is nothing mechanical or forced about life; one thing always flows naturally from another.

---

4   *Yeshayah* 3:10.

5   The *Maharal* explains that this is in distinction to animals, which are called *beheimah*—the same letters as בה מה, which means, "its essence is already in it." Their entire potential is already present at the moment they come into being; there is no real growth.

6   Perhaps this is included in *Rashi's* statement (*Bereishis* 6:9) that the "progeny" of the righteous are mitzvos and good deeds. Instead of artificial acts, true Divine service is to spring forth naturally. Perhaps, furthermore, it is no coincidence that Adam's original task was to "work and guard" the Garden of Eden (*Bereishis* 2:15). The *Zohar* (*Tikkunei Zohar*, 55) interprets "working" the garden as referring to the positive mitzvos, while "guarding" it refers to abstaining from the negative commandments. Even assuming that this is entirely a metaphor, the very fact that mitzvah observance could be even metaphorically referred to as "working the garden" is testament to the fact that Divine service is to come forth naturally, like plants in a garden. Note further that after Hashem "sprouts all manners of trees" in the garden, He places Adam there to tend to it, effectively continuing Hashem's own program of planting the trees.

Encountering Torah in this framework puts all our strivings into a context of authentic growth that sprouts naturally from the person like foliage from the ground.

By putting Torah into this context, the Minim allow us to see Torah and mitzvos not as something artificially superimposed onto "life," but instead, as something that emerges organically from life itself.[7]

Details, Revisited

Let us review some of the basic guidelines of this mitzvah within the framework of the life connection.

In chapter two, we suggested that at its most basic sense, what the Torah asks of us is to take the Arba Minim and simply spend time with them. Spending time with plant life allows one to feel and connect to the life within them. In order to truly identify with, and become aware of, the life force flowing through them, it is necessary to make them the centerpiece; to bond with them and to become enmeshed with them. The more one allows oneself to identify with and see oneself within the Minim, the stronger the feeling of aliveness, and the more central their property of vivacity becomes.

At the simplest level, the unique commandment of physically "taking" the Minim is to facilitate a connection and association with life, which in turn allows for a greater association of Hashem, Torah, and the Jewish People with life. Perhaps at a deeper level it can be understood as an act of taking aliveness to oneself; of making it a part of oneself and incorporating it into one's personality.

To the extent that the Minim are living things that are "taken" by oneself, perhaps they are to be viewed and sensed as an actual part of oneself. In a sense, it is as if each Jew individually, and the Jewish People as a whole, sprouts and blossoms, coming to life on Sukkos, the summit of our yearly journey.[8]

---

7   It is interesting to contemplate the word "Lulav," which is used to refer to the palm bough. Its root would appear to be the same as that of the word "*livluv*," which means "sprouting" or "blossoming."

8   If we "blossom" on Sukkos, what is it that is blossoming? Perhaps, all of the spiritual work we put in during the year is now blossoming and coming alive through the Minim. The life

Waving

We shake and move the species around. Movement expresses life; essentially, we are experiencing and expressing life in the presence of the Source of life.

We shake the species in every direction—right, behind, left, front, up, and down. As the Gemara explains, we shake them in numerous directions before He to Whom belong the four directions.[9] We draw life from its source and suffuse the world with it. In a sense, we are recreating the world within which we live and function, as one of life.

Yours

One must own the Minim in order to fulfill the mitzvah. The identification necessary in order to sense the life force flowing through the Minim necessitates ownership. I more readily relate to my own property.

Going deeper, this touches upon the uniquely personal nature of life itself. Life must be experienced as one's own. It is a subjective experience.

This personal connection with the life of the Minim, of course, impacts the aliveness then injected into one's relationship with Torah and mitzvos. If we are to truly sense Torah as a living entity, we need to develop our own vibrant connection with it; to find our unique niche within the totality of Torah.

Hadar

Where does *hadar* fit in within the framework of focusing on life? For one thing, it facilitates our relating to and identifying with the Minim and their vivacity. It attracts us to them and causes us to wish to connect with them.

---

force flowing through all of the mitzvos and the Divine service done throughout the year is crystallized into the life force of the Minim, and with this aliveness we stand before Hashem and praise Him.

(This parallels our discussion of *hiddur mitzvah*, where we suggested that through the mitzvos we beautify ourselves, with the accumulated beauty expressing itself in the beauty of the Minim with which we adorn ourselves.)

9   *Sukkah* 38a.

At a somewhat deeper level, though, the beauty of the species brings out their vivacity. Beauty itself is an expression of vitality and makes us feel more alive. *Hadar* is an expression of the inner life of the thing.

Perhaps life by itself is inherently beautiful, unless corrupted by something less than beautiful.

Rejoicing before God

The essence of this mitzvah is that of rejoicing, but we rejoice with items that convey and express aliveness. Where and how does the joy and aliveness come together? What is the relationship between joy, the stated essence of this mitzvah, and life?

At an extremely simple level, joy animates and deepens the experience of aliveness. For the Minim to have their desired effect on us, we must relate to them, and we are more able to relate to that which is outside of ourselves when we are in a state of joy.

Going deeper, joy, by definition, is the subjective experience of the objective reality called life.

Anything that brings joy, real or imagined, is because it brings about an enhanced sense of aliveness, real or imagined. Negative feelings arise from being connected to the things that block a person from realizing his aliveness.

Since human life, the highest and most sophisticated form of life, must be self-generated, true and lasting joy is achieved when we activate ourselves and generate our own existence.

Joy and life, then, are one and the same, with the former being simply an external, subjective expression of the latter. In a sense, when the Torah instructs us to "rejoice before God," it is telling us to "truly experience your aliveness in the presence of the source of that aliveness."

The Mikdash

The full, seven-day mitzvah of the Arba Minim applies specifically in the Mikdash. The Mikdash is referred to in numerous places throughout the siddur as *Beis Chayeinu*, the center of our life. In *Tehillim*, (133:3) concerning "the mountains of Zion," we read, "for there did Hashem command the blessing, life unto forever." The Mikdash is the place from which life emanates, and it is there that we go to celebrate our connection to true life and its source. In the Mikdash, the Jewish People in its entirety "comes to life" by taking the species and becoming one with them.

Anshei Yerushalayim

Earlier, we noted the practice of the people of Yerushalayim to carry the Minim around with them throughout Sukkos. We suggested that this optimal fulfillment allowed the Minim to color all aspects of their lives for the week of Sukkos. Looking at this from the perspective of engaging life, we might say that this ongoing engagement allowed them to conceive of Hashem, Torah, and mitzvos in a different light, seeing an entire construct designed to seek and bestow life. Through the on-going presence of the Minim, they were able to see every encounter with Hashem as an encounter with the living God. It allowed them to perceive God as first and foremost the epitome and source of life. It further allowed them to see the greater whole of the Jewish People as one of a truly alive nation. And it allowed them to see the whole of Torah as the true path of life.

More specifically, the Minim allowed and prompted them to revisit all aspects of Torah and *avodah* and contemplate how they revolve around aliveness and how they must be infused with the quest for life. It allowed them to see each mitzvah as a living entity, urging them to seek out the spark of life in every mitzvah.

Although this degree of involvement with the Minim may not be available to us, the model is clear, and there is certainly room for raising our own level of engagement and taking full advantage of the "living species."

Hallel

As we discussed earlier, the main activity performed with the Minim is that of reciting *Hallel*. Let us now view this activity within the context of the Minim as symbols of life.

Before even examining the themes of *Hallel*, let us examine the general themes of *Tehillim* itself. Life and death, for David and for Klal

Yisrael, are very pervasive themes throughout *Tehillim*, both explicitly and in other terms.

The Midrash states that Adam HaRishon, who was to live one thousand years, was shown that David HaMelech would live only three hours.[10] He asked to donate seventy years of his life to David, who in fact lived seventy years. Essentially, then, David's entire life was a novelty. In fact, the book of *Tehillim* culminates in the verse, "Let everything that breathes"—i.e., life itself—"praise God." As the Midrash comments on this very verse, we must praise God for each and every breath; otherwise put, for each and every connection with life.

Celebrating Aliveness

If this is true of *Tehillim* in general, in *Hallel* this focus becomes even more pronounced. "The dead cannot praise God,"[11] "I was surrounded by the travails of death, and the straits of *she'ol* attacked me...Hashem heard my cry,"[12] "For You have saved my soul from death, my foot from stumbling,"[13] "I shall walk before Hashem in the lands of the living,"[14] "Precious in the eyes of God is the death of the pious ones,"[15] "I will not die but will live! Hashem has visited me with suffering, but unto death He has not given me."[16] *Hallel* is essentially a celebration of life as received from the Giver and Generator of life.

The root of all praise we can utter before Hashem is praising Him for the gift of life itself. The most basic generosity Hashem bestows upon us is that of life, with any additions adding to the "quality of life," making us more and more alive. Ultimately, whenever we praise God, we are praising Him for life itself.

The Minim, with their life and vibrance, are the perfect tools with which to express *Hallel*.

---

10   *Yalkut Shimoni, Bereishis* 41.
11   *Tehillim* 115:17.
12   Ibid., 116:3–4.
13   Ibid., 116:8.
14   Ibid., 116:9.
15   Ibid., 116:15.
16   Ibid., 118:17.

A Unique *Hallel*

Life is a prominent theme within *Hallel*, but especially so with the *Hallel* of Sukkos. The *Hallel* recited on Sukkos, coming on the heels of Rosh Hashanah and Yom Kippur, is an expression of praise over being inscribed in the Book of Life. We take life itself to praise Hashem for a new lease on life.

"The created nation will praise God." The Midrash explains that this is a reference to the nation that is (re)created on Rosh Hashanah, who then goes on to praise Hashem on Sukkos through the reciting of the *Hallel*.[17] Unlike the *Hallel* recited on other occasions, the *Hallel* of Sukkos is recited not over a specific miracle or event, but for the gift of life itself.

Hodu La'Hashem Ki Tov

We hold the Minim throughout the entire *Hallel*, but the primary waving and shaking is done when reciting the words "Thank Hashem, for He is good; for forever is His kindness." Much of *Hallel* focuses on specific things for which we thank Hashem, but this phrase does not focus on any particular kindness, instead generalizes Hashem's *chessed*.

Utilizing the Minim

Having examined the idea of life as a major theme of *Hallel*, let us contemplate the use of the Arba Minim while saying *Hallel*. How does this upgrade our *Hallel* experience? What depth do the Minim bring to our recital of *Hallel*?

If, as we said, *Hallel* is all about thanksgiving for life, we may need something that can help us break through the layers that prevent us from feeling and expressing that gratitude, whether they be those of cynicism, taking things for granted, or negativity. The Minim, with their aliveness, freshness, and beauty, chip away just a little bit at these layers. Joining the spark of life evinced by the Minim can help identify the goodness in one's life. Even someone who is in a difficult situation can find some sliver of goodness in life, something for which to be

---

17   *Vayikra Rabbah* 30:3.

grateful, some real aliveness. The Minim can help discover that there is a spark of gratitude and aliveness even in just being alive.[18]

A true recognition of our own aliveness wells up into a true recognition of God as the "God of life." The Minim help us make that association and truly feel the fact that Hashem is *Elokim chaim*.

וכל החיים יודוך סלה—לפי שאנו חיים ואתה חי מודים חי אנחנו לך.

"And all *the living* shall worship You"[19] (*Modim* prayer)—we are alive, and You are alive, and so we bow to You.

Avudraham, p. 203

Earlier, we discussed the fact that the story of mankind, and that of the universe, is the search for life. Beginning with Adam and Chavah in Gan Eden and continuing through the ultimate goal of *techiyas ha'meisim* with everything that entails—this is the central theme of the Torah. These are lofty and abstract concepts. The mitzvah of engaging and rejoicing with the Arba Minim, though, allows these realities to filter into our consciousness in the most tangible way. On Sukkos, we literally hold in our hands the life we seek. It becomes our companion, our instrument of celebration, our centerpiece.

On Sukkos, when we reach the summit of our journey, we are able to touch a modicum of this true life, this transcendence of death. As we saw in an earlier section, Rav Acha Bar Yaakov, while shaking his Lulav, would declare, "a spear in the eye of the Satan!" The Satan, we are told, is himself the Angel of Death.[20] On Sukkos, as expressed by the Minim, we escape the clutches of the Angel of Death. With our appreciation of

---

18   This might require advance preparation. A suggested exercise is to think in advance of something in your life for which you are grateful, or that makes you feel particularly alive in a real way. When you hold and wave the Minim, have that particular thing in mind. While waving the Minim during the recital of the words "thank Hashem, for He is good," etc., have that blessing in mind as an expression of Hashem's goodness and as His being the source of all life.

19   *Avudraham* interprets *"modim"* as prostrating oneself before God.

20   *Bava Basra* 16a.

the meaning and purpose of Torah and mitzvos, our Lulav truly represents the triumph over death.

Summation

Life is both the starting point and the end point. It is the simple commodity of life itself that everything else is built upon, but at the same time it is the attainment of true life, in its highest and most authentic form, that is our ultimate objective. This is the cycle of the *Regalim* that culminates in Sukkos and then begins again. At the end of our journey we reach life, and from that life we start again, hoping to complete the cycle once more at an even more elevated level.

The Path of Life

King David declares before God, "You will teach me the path of life; in Your presence is the fullness of joy."[21] The word used for "fullness" is *sova*. The Midrash comments that the letters forming *sova* can also be read as *sheva* (seven), and that this is a reference to the seven mitzvos of Sukkos: the sukkah, each of the Arba Minim, the *chagigah* offering, and the general mitzvah of rejoicing on Sukkos.[22] These seven items together create the full framework of Sukkos, when we reach the fullness of joy before God's countenance. It is illuminating to notice that the beginning of that very verse focuses on "the path of life." The search for life culminates in the rejoicing in front of God's countenance with the very objects that symbolize life itself.[23]

Tying It All together

We have looked at three aspects of the mitzvah of the Arba Minim: joy, *hiddur*, and *chaim*. In a previous segment we discussed the possible connections between joy and *chaim*. Is there any connection between the three commodities? What, if anything, is the relationship between them?

---

21 *Tehillim* 16:11.

22 *Vayikra Rabbah* 30:2.

23 Another connection to life is that the numerical value of Lulav is the same as *chaim*. We perform eighteen shakings with the Lulav each time—*chai*. And kabbalistically, the name represented by the Lulav is *Kel Chai*—it's all about *chiyus*.

We began with joy. Joy is a subjective emotional state. What is the source of true joy? True human joy is experienced when a person feels that he has attained something noble, something lofty, something of true beauty. It thus emerges that joy is a *subjective* expression of having attained the *objective* state of *hadar*. True joy, then, is the outer layer of its root, which is *hadar*; true joy gives way to *hadar*.

Hadar, itself, though, is an expression of something deeper. It is an expression of *chaim*. Adam HaRishon, who was created to be immortal, shone with *hadar*; when he lost his immortality, he lost his beauty and splendor as well.[24] Beauty and *hadar* are themselves only manifestations of something deeper, aliveness itself.[25]

It is interesting that the Torah's presentation of this mitzvah seems to mirror the three levels of depth. We have suggested that the most external level of the mitzvah is that of *simchah*; deeper is *hadar*; and deeper still is *chaim*. The Torah explicitly defines the mitzvah as one of *simchah*. It never commands us about *hadar* per se, but suggestively places the concept of *hadar*, which it at least mentions by name, in a place of prominence of the mitzvah. The concept of *chaim*, on the other hand, is not even mentioned by name, but is present in the background.

---

24   *Bereishis Rabbah* 12:6.
25   At the deepest level, joy is a manifestation of life. *Netziv* writes (*Haamek Davar, Bereishis* 23:1, as well as in the numerous sources referenced there) that the word "*chaim*" throughout *Tanach* is used with two distinct meanings: At times it refers to life per se, but at times it is used to refer to joy and happiness.

Epilogue

In the opening pages of our search, we posited that the mitzvah of the Arba Minim, which is the defining activity of Sukkos, itself the climax of the entire yearly cycle, might carry messages integral to understanding the totality of our mission. Looking back, we have discovered that indeed, this mitzvah touches upon some of the most basic ideas underlying Torah and mitzvos: The various forms of joy that are to accompany all of our mitzvos and Divine service; the spiritual beauty achieved through Torah life; and the life and vivacity so central to all of Torah.

Each mitzvah is an entire way of life distilled into an action. A mitzvah does not begin and end with its technical execution. Part of the effect a mitzvah has on us is through learning it, immersing oneself in it, and living it throughout the year.

The Torah states, "These are the mitzvos that a person shall do and live through them."[1] The Torah expects us to live each mitzvah; to use each and every mitzvah to mold and shape our lives.

We discover ourselves in the mitzvah. The mitzvah helps us discover our inner reality; it helps us understand who we are. The mitzvah of the Arba Minim, properly fulfilled, opens up for us our inner reservoirs of joy in all of its manifestations, and demonstrates to us how all of those forms of joy can connect us to our Creator. It reminds us that we are able

---

1   *Vayikra* 18:5.

to—indeed designed to—achieve inner beauty through our service of Hashem and Divinely ordered character refinement. And, perhaps most importantly, it allows us to actualize ourselves as living beings created specifically for the purpose of attaching ourselves to the living God.

בְּאוֹר פְּנֵי מֶלֶךְ חַיִּים.

In the light of the King's countenance is life.

Mishlei 16:15

Appendix
Getting Practical

Practice Runs

Rav Zundel of Salant, the mentor of Rav Yisrael Salanter, founder of the Mussar Movement, was once discovered in the pre-dawn hours of the first night of Sukkos, holding his Arba Minim and performing the *naanu'im*, the waving and shaking that are to be done with them. This aroused the surprise of those who discovered him, since the mitzvah does not actually begin until the next morning! When asked, Rav Zundel explained that he was practicing the *naanu'im*! "Members of the military practice their skills daily, even if they are already quite proficient, in order to ensure perfection. We should do the same in our Divine service, so as to ensure that our every move is appropriate."[1]

Based on what we have seen about the purpose and character of the mitzvah of the Arba Minim, perhaps we may suggest that there is another aspect that could, at least theoretically, be practiced. The various species are supposed to evoke different emotional reactions, which are then to be harnessed in service of Hashem, but it may take some getting used to for them to have the proper effect. Imagine

---

1   *Tenuas Hamussar*, p. 153.

practicing in advance, while using the opportunity to appreciate the unique appearance and properties of each species.

Inasmuch as each species has its own unique form of joy, it might even be beneficial to practice with one species at a time, tuning in to the unique mood evoked by that species. Then, one can experiment with the various combinations, and how they interact with each other, until finally putting all four together and capturing the unique flavor of the complete package.

Getting into the Swing of Things

Practice runs may be helpful, but perhaps there is another activity that is even more integral to proper and robust fulfillment of this mitzvah.

The species, we have suggested, have been carefully selected and chosen by our Creator as those that facilitate maximal, and specifically desirable, forms of spiritual joy. But their ability to do so depends largely on the effect they are to have on our psyche. We have already discussed some prerequisites for this effect; let us explore another.

Especially in our urban communities, and to an even stronger degree, with our new virtual reality, we live a life largely divorced from the nature where the species grow. The result of this is that we look at a Lulav and see nothing but a religious artifact used on the holiday of Sukkos, and the same for the other three species. In this way our species are sterilized and isolated from their natural habitat, losing their context, which is a major part of their significance.

A Lulav divorced from its place at the center of a palm tree is not a real Lulav. Someone intimately acquainted with palms sees the Lulav in its natural habitat whenever and wherever he sees it. The same is true of the Esrog and Hadassim, and most certainly of the Aravos, whose very significance is their ability to conjure the image of their proximity to water. To properly fulfill this mitzvah, we need to regain a sense of the beauty and wondrousness of nature.

The need to familiarize ourselves with the host trees becomes even more acute if, as we have suggested, the trees themselves play such a major role in the execution of the mitzvah.

Perhaps part of a full and robust fulfillment of this mitzvah is that of learning to recognize and appreciate the host trees of the species. This means taking the time to identify the trees, getting to know them and even developing a relationship with them. The deeper the relationship we have with these trees, the more we bring into our act of taking up the species.

Preparation for a Mitzvah

Every mitzvah has its own mood, feeling, and ambience; every mitzvah requires a prior investment of time and thought and work. The mitzvah of Lulav, of course, is no different.

There is a unique difficulty that presents itself in attempting to prepare adequately for the mitzvah of the Arba Minim. Consider the difference between preparations for Pesach and those of Sukkos. From immediately after Purim, people go into Pesach mode. Certainly, once the beginning of the month of Nissan has arrived, Pesach is on our radar screens, and we feel the need to learn more about it, its mitzvos, and how to fulfill them optimally. We (hopefully) arrive at the Seder with many hours of learning and mental preparation under our belts.

The same cannot usually be said for Sukkos, following as it does immediately on the heels of Yom Kippur and the entire Elul, Rosh Hashanah, and Aseres Yemei Teshuvah season. Suddenly and without warning, we find ourselves deposited on the doorstep of Sukkos, with much to do within a frantically short period of time. Who has time to prepare mentally?

Surely, however, there must be a way of getting around this problem. We must find a way of remembering that there is life after Rosh Hashanah and Yom Kippur, and that when those days have passed, in all likelihood we will find ourselves staring Sukkos in the face. For those of us who feel that even thinking about Sukkos during the days of awe detracts from the solemnity of those days, perhaps we can try preparing even before the advent of Rosh Hashanah or, for that matter, of Elul! And inasmuch as Sukkos is a natural outgrowth of the *Yamim Nora'im* season, if done properly our experience of the days of awe stands only to gain by looking at the whole picture, including Sukkos.

Halachah makes it clear that we are not to treat Sukkos as some surprise visitor that suddenly falls upon us after Yom Kippur. According to *Rashi*, one is obligated to begin studying the laws of Sukkos a full thirty days before its arrival, and all agree that once that period has begun, there is assumed to be at least a subconscious awareness of its proximity.

The *Chayei Adam* writes about the importance of taking the time to prepare for a mitzvah.[2] He writes that in his own personal experience, a mitzvah performed after preparing mentally for it is qualitatively different from one performed without such preparation. This is true at the micro-level—that of pausing immediately before performing a mitzvah in order to reflect and prepare—but also at the macro-level—that of taking note of an approaching mitzvah and taking steps to mentally and spiritually prepare oneself for its proper performance.

Spending Time with the Species

Performance of the mitzvah of the Arba Minim along the lines that we have elucidated, requires engaging with them in more than simply a perfunctory manner. As we have suggested, the mitzvah involves "taking" the Minim and allowing them to have an impact on one's psyche. The Minim must belong to the person, we suggested, because it is necessary to have a relationship with them. While one would certainly discharge the obligation simply by lifting the Minim, and most certainly if one also waved them, optimal fulfillment would seemingly require a more immersive and focused engagement. Let's make sure we are truly spending quality time with them!

It is not always easy to arrange for such an experience, but with some foresight and planning it can be achieved.

Part of this might be taking full advantage of reciting *Hallel* with the Minim. Although the Minim are only shaken at specific junctures throughout *Hallel*, in truth we recite the entire *Hallel* with the Minim. Clearly, there is significance to simply having the Minim in hand during the recital of *Hallel*. The simple act of holding the Minim at that time

---

2   *Chayei Adam* 68:28.

contributes to and enhances the reciting of *Hallel*. *Hallel* is therefore an opportune time to invest in a robust fulfillment of this mitzvah.

Put Some Dance into Your Step

If a perfunctory act of taking the Minim is less than an optimal fulfillment of the mitzvah, the same is certainly true of the waving of the Minim. If, as we have seen, the very raison d'etre of waving the species is that of expressing joy, it stands to reason that this should be done in a manner that could at least somehow be construed as such! If you look around carefully, you will notice some people clandestinely rocking on their heels while shaking the Minim. It is indeed possible to put some spirit in one's waving without making a public spectacle of himself.

Without Anxiety

Each mitzvah, and certainly each Yom Tov, brings with it the opportunity for growth, but, approached with an unhealthy attitude, can lead to frustration and vexation. This mitzvah is no different, and we need to do our best to approach it in an optimal way.

Here are some suggestions to make sure we make it through Sukkos and the Arba Minim without unnecessary stress.

Take It Easy

Although we have suggested some practical ways to enhance the practical performance of this mitzvah, it is important not to overly focus on a perfect execution of it. We are not machines, and we cannot always control our inner experience. The belief that we must produce on demand a specific emotional reaction and experience can lead to frustration.

As we have mentioned repeatedly, mitzvos in general are not limited to the brief moments of their fulfillment. If we have invested time, thought, and effort in understanding the mitzvah and its messages, we have utilized the mitzvah properly no matter what our experience is at the specific moment of its performance.

Keep Your Eyes to Yourself

It is tempting to eye the specimens of your neighbor in shul. This should be avoided, though. The Hadassim also look greener, the

Aravos fresher, the Esrog yellower, and the Lulav straighter on the other side of the table. If you have seen someone else's specimens and have entered into a whirlpool of self-doubt and existential angst, be aware that chances are that that very person has seen *your* samples and is now going through the same struggle. Your specimens are fine just as they are.

In fact, you might want to avoid gazing too closely even at your own specimens, lest you discover some new flaw you hadn't noticed originally.

Ignore the Naysayers

Beware of those who see it as their mission to convince you of the inferiority of your specimens. Humor them, but do not take their words too seriously.

Beauty in the Eyes of the Beholder

We have spoken much of the beauty of the Arba Minim. Let's acknowledge, though, that it's not always easy—or within our ability—to procure a truly stunning specimen. Our Esrog might have an interesting shape; our Lulav might be less than impressive. This is not cause for concern. We need not be perfectionists when it comes to this mitzvah. No matter how your specimen looks, it has some beauty; focus on that, not how it could have been nicer looking. Perhaps this is training for learning to see the beauty in ourselves and others. At any rate, we have suggested that a significant component in taking the Minim is that of their host trees; any lack of beauty in the specimens themselves can be compensated by focusing one's thoughts on the trees, or on the species as a whole.

Tending to the Arba Minim

The species require care throughout the holiday in order to maintain their freshness and viability. This can be looked at as a boring and time-consuming chore, or as an opportunity for growth on several levels.

First, and most simply, it is, of course, part of the mitzvah. The time and effort spent on maintenance and care of the species is time spent on proper performance of a mitzvah.

Going further, it is a chance to nurture one's relationship with the species. As we have suggested earlier, the requirement for ownership of the Arba Minim might be an indication of the need for a personal relationship with them as our representatives and even extensions of ourselves.

Developing a relationship takes time and investment. The first stage of the courtship between shaker and species might be the initial steps of procuring the set, whether that constitutes ordering a set or actively searching for just the right samples.

These initial steps set the stage for a relationship, but the actual growing of the relationship requires time and care. The next step is tending to the Lulav's needs, dressing it, keeping it fresh, fixing the rings, and so on. These acts foster a deeper relationship with the species. They also afford the ability and opportunity to spend "quality time" with them, noticing their beauty and natural charm, and, of course, vivacity.

Shemini Atzeres

Many people have had the experience of feeling a letdown on Shemini Atzeres. After spending six days reciting *Hallel* with the Arba Minim, suddenly we recite *Hallel* with empty hands. The irony is that Shemini Atzeres is supposed to be the time of the greatest joy!

We can suggest the following approach. As we have proposed in an earlier chapter, part of "taking the species to yourself" is taking them "into yourself." We are to make them a part of ourselves. If that is true, then when we arrive at Shemini Atzeres, the values and qualities of the Arba Minim have been brought into the person himself! The *hadar*, the vitality, the beauty, symmetry, exuberant joy—everything expressed by the species—is now permanently installed in the person to the extent that it is no longer necessary to utilize physical items to evoke and bring out these qualities.

In fact, awareness that we are going to recite *Hallel* on Shemini Atzeres without the Minim should force us to utilize the Minim in such a manner that it is not just an experience, but rather one is imbuing oneself with these values, qualities, and concepts.

What about the *Hallel* recited on Pesach and Shavuos? Isn't it missing the crucial ingredient of the Arba Minim? The truth is that it *is* missing. A full, robust *Hallel* does indeed call for the Arba Minim! But Pesach and Shavuos are just stepping-stones on the way to Sukkos. They are part of the process. We are not ready yet at that time for the Arba Minim. It is only on Sukkos that we recite *Hallel* in its fullest and most authentic sense.

About the Author

Binyamin Feldman, originally of Atlanta, Georgia, lives with his family in Yerushalayim, where he is involved in studying, editing, and teaching in Torah institutions. He welcomes comments and general feedback and can be contacted at Livinglulav@gmail.com.